Table of Contents

Habitual Mastery

Turn Routines into Reality

by

Dr. ant

Contents

Introduction

At the heart of every action you take lies a habit. Whether intentional or not, these repetitive behaviors play a significant role in shaping your daily life, threading the fabric of who you are. The beauty of habits lies in their dual nature: they can either propel you toward success or silently tether you to routines that no longer serve you. Our exploration begins here, at the crux of awareness and potential, inviting you to embark on a journey toward understanding and mastering your habits for profound personal growth.

There's a certain magic to habits—the way they weave themselves into the tapestry of our lives, often without conscious decision. From the moment you rise to how you wind down each evening, habits dictate a vast portion of your day. You develop them not because you've consciously chosen them, but often because they provide immediate utility or comfort. But what if you could mold this magic, harness these invisible threads, and turn them into strings that play the symphonies of a life well-lived?

Understanding your habits is akin to holding a mirror up to your lifestyle. It requires a frank and empathetic self-assessment. What routines define you? Which behaviors have you unconsciously adopted? As we navigate through this book, you'll learn to observe these patterns with clarity and compassion. Not every habit ingrained in your life serves a beneficial purpose, yet each can teach you something about your priorities, motivations, and the changes you ought to make.

The path of habit transformation is neither straight nor narrow. It presents twists and turns, demanding a scientist's curiosity and an artist's courage. Change begins not with grand gestures but with simple, deliberate efforts. Each chapter will guide you step-by-step, providing the tools and insights necessary for lasting change. The journey might require patience, but the rewards—a profound sense of empowerment and potential—are worth every effort.

You'll discover that the science of changing habits is rooted in an intricate dance between neurology and psychology. We'll explore how minor shifts in mindset and approach can trigger significant transformations. Your environment, too, plays a pivotal role. Are your surroundings conducive to the habits you wish to foster? You'll learn to curate a space brimming with positivity and support.

The battle against internal resistance is a common yet conquerable hurdle. Inside you, doubts and fears may whisper that your goals are unreachable. Yet, with strategies tailored for overcoming such internal conflicts, you'll equip yourself not only to tackle these challenges but to emerge victorious. Remember, persistence isn't just about persistence itself; it's about nurturing motivation, even on days when resolve wavers.

Personal growth doesn't happen in isolation; it's influenced by the social circles you keep and the cultural milieu you dwell in. Understanding how to navigate these influences turns potential hindrances into allies in your journey. Peer support can be harnessed for positive reinforcement, while detrimental influences can be skillfully minimized or transformed.

Perhaps one of the most empowering aspects of this journey is the knowledge that setbacks are not failures but stepping stones. You'll learn to approach lapses not with dismay but with a strategic mindset that promotes rebound and recovery. Each stumble offers a lesson, an opportunity for deeper understanding and even more significant progress.

As you progress, tracking and adjusting your habits will become second nature. The right tools empower you to monitor and fine-tune your routines, setting the stage for long-term sustainability and adaptation. The goal is not just to build habits but to maintain and adapt them over time, ensuring they continue to serve you as life evolves.

This book is a tapestry woven with the wisdom of personal narratives, illustrative of both success and learning curves. These stories illuminate the challenges and triumphs others have faced, offering insights that transcend their lives and resonate with yours. Through these narratives, you'll find inspiration and practical lessons that add depth and relevance to your journey.

In entering this exploration of habit mastery, you take the first step not just toward personal transformation but toward a fuller understanding of who you are and who you can become. It's an invitation to chart a course that aligns your habits with your deepest personal goals and aspirations, ultimately crafting a lifestyle that resonates with purpose and fulfillment.

Chapter 1: Understanding Habits

Habits are the invisible architecture of our daily lives, guiding us with ease or ensnaring us in cycles we'd rather break. To truly harness their power, it's essential to dive into the nature of habits, understanding not just their mechanics but the subtle ways they shape who we are and who we wish to become. Habits often operate below the radar of our conscious thought, providing comfort in their predictability, yet challenging us when they conflict with our aspirations. By recognizing how they function, we can better navigate the intricate dance between routine and change, crafting pathways that lead us toward personal growth and enhanced productivity. Awareness is the first step on this journey, opening doors to a transformative understanding of our behavioral patterns and the potential within us all to evolve deliberately and joyfully.

The Psychology of Habit Formation

Understanding the psychology behind habit formation is a crucial first step in shaping our behaviors towards personal growth and enhanced productivity. At its core, a habit is a behavior that has been repeated enough times to become automatic. This automaticity is born out of a neurological loop consisting of three main components: a cue, a routine, and a reward. While this pattern might sound simple, it reveals profound insights about how our brains enable us to operate efficiently, often under the radar of our conscious thoughts.

The process of forming habits begins with a *cue*—an external trigger that tells the brain to go into autopilot mode and which habit to use. Think about the buzz of the alarm clock in the morning. It's a simple sound, but it acts as a powerful cue to your brain that it's time to follow your morning routine, whether that's to hit snooze, stretch, or grab a cup of coffee. How we respond to these cues—essentially, the habits we form—can be influenced by the psychological framework laid down by our past experiences, environment, and personality traits.

Next is the *routine*, which is the behavior itself. This is the action or series of actions triggered by the cue. Routines can encompass anything from exercise to eating habits or even checking your phone. The routine is what we think of as the habit itself, the action that takes place repeatedly. What's intriguing is how the routine encompasses both beneficial and harmful patterns. Developing an awareness of these routines through introspection and observation can empower individuals to redesign them consciously.

The last component is the *reward*. Once the routine is complete, the brain receives some form of reward. This reward can be tangible or emotional, such as feelings of achievement, satisfaction, or relaxation. The brain's pleasure centers are engaged by these rewards, which reinforces the habit loop. Over time, this loop solidifies, driving the automaticity of the habit. The anticipation of the reward becomes associated with the cue, creating a powerful neurological craving, making habits incredibly difficult to change without deliberate effort.

Psychologists suggest that the challenge of altering a habit lies in maintaining the initial cue and the ultimate reward, while changing the routine itself—in other words, substituting a negative behavior with a positive one that provides a similar reward. This approach requires not just willpower, but also a strategic understanding of the habit loop. Recognizing the cues and rewards can help reframe the routine in a way that aligns with personal growth goals.

Moreover, the environment plays an unsung role in shaping our habits. Our surroundings often dictate the cues we encounter, which can trigger our habits without us realizing it. For example, having a bowl of fresh fruit visible on the counter can cue an individual to opt for healthier snacks more frequently than if they were hidden away in the pantry. Simple environmental tweaks can harness the psychology of habit formation to redirect behaviors effortlessly.

Our belief system also has a powerful influence on our habits. Belief is the catalyst that gives us the confidence to change persistent patterns. Research shows that believing in the possibility of change, often driven by community support or personal conviction, can significantly bolster our ability to form new habits. When challenges disrupt our routines, those with the belief that they can adapt and improve are more likely to stay the course.

Community and social networks can profoundly impact the habit formation process. Often, our social circles shape what we perceive as normal and aspirational. Surrounding oneself with individuals who embody the habits one wishes to cultivate can provide a framework for success through observational learning and shared motivation. Social dynamics often reinforce certain cues and rewards, making some routines more attractive or viable.

Emotional resilience is another critical factor in understanding habit formation. Emotions have a direct impact on the habits we prioritize or neglect. In times of stress or discomfort, individuals might revert to unhealthy habits as a coping mechanism because they offer immediate comfort or familiarity. Cultivating resilience involves developing the capacity to recognize these emotional cues and respond with healthier routines, ultimately changing one's emotional landscape over time.

In conclusion, the psychology of habit formation is a dynamic interplay between mental, emotional, and social elements. Understanding this process gives us the tools to not only identify our habits but also to transform them. It is not just about rewriting the script of our routines, but also about enhancing self-awareness and nurturing a mindset open to change. In this intricate dance between cue, routine, and reward, lies the potential for profound personal development.

As we embark on the journey of self-improvement, embracing the complexity of habit formation can empower us to take control of our behaviors. Through this awareness, we're not just changing what we do, but we're also changing who we become, paving the way for lasting transformation.

The Role of Habits in Daily Life

Habits are the invisible architecture of our daily lives. They shape our actions, define our routines, and often dictate the rhythm of our days. From the moment we wake up to the time we fall asleep, habits provide a framework that governs how we interact with the world. Understanding these patterns of behavior offers us a gateway to consciously shape our lives, but also demands an awareness of their power and influence.

One of the most significant aspects of habits is their ability to operate automatically, allowing us to conserve mental energy for more complex tasks. Have you ever found yourself driving home only to realize you barely remember any details of the journey? That's the power of habitual behavior at work. Our brains, ever keen on finding efficiencies, prefer this autopilot mode. It's why, despite our best intentions, we find ourselves scrolling through our phones or reaching for snacks without a second thought.

But habits are more than just shortcuts for our brain. They serve as the foundation upon which personal growth and productivity are built. Embracing positive habits can be transformative, enabling us to harness potential that might otherwise remain dormant. They equip us with the discipline to set aside time for exercise, the courage to tackle challenging tasks, and the perseverance to pursue lifelong learning and self-improvement.

Consider the morning routines of some of the most accomplished individuals. Many share common elements such as meditation, exercise, or reading. These aren't mere coincidences but are intentional habits designed to start their days with focus and energy. By embedding beneficial habits into our daily lives, we set the stage for success long before any specific task begins.

However, understanding the role of habits also means recognizing their potential to entrench less desirable behaviors. Negative habits can stealthily root themselves, drawing us into patterns like procrastination, overeating, or excessive screen time. These behaviors can snowball, adversely affecting our well-being and productivity. Awareness is the first step toward change. By identifying these habits, we open doors to redesigning our routine to better serve our aspirations.

The real magic happens when we realize that habits aren't rigid. They are remarkably adaptable, capable of transformation with deliberate effort. Small, incremental changes can have profound effects over time. For instance, replacing just thirty minutes of social media with reading each day can lead to the completion of numerous books over a year, expanding our knowledge and perspective with minimal disruption to our routine.

Moreover, habits extend beyond individual pursuits; they influence our social connections and professional environments. In the workplace, good habits can foster a culture of efficiency and innovation. On a personal level, they impact how we nurture relationships and manage our time with loved ones. When shared, habits like volunteering, exercising, or cooking together can strengthen bonds and build communities grounded in shared values and experiences.

Crafting habits aligned with our values requires introspection and commitment. It demands an understanding of what truly matters to us, what we seek to achieve, and who we aspire to become. Once we have clarity on these fronts, habits become powerful tools that drive our daily actions towards our long-term goals.

However, the transformative journey of habit formation is not linear. Setbacks are inevitable, and motivation fluctuates. What distinguishes those who succeed is resilience and a willingness to view each stumble as a learning opportunity. In these moments, stepping back to reevaluate our habits can provide insights necessary for effective adjustment and sustainable implementation.

At the heart of shaping habits lies the belief in our capacity to change. It's an acknowledgment that even entrenched patterns, once thought immovable, can be altered with patience and perseverance. It's about rewriting our story, one habit at a time, in the pursuit of a life that resonates with our deepest aspirations. And so, our daily habits, once understood and skillfully managed, become not just actions but a testament to who we are and who we are becoming.

Chapter 2: Identifying Your Current Patterns

Understanding the journey of personal growth begins with a clear view of where we stand today. Developing an awareness of our existing habits is like looking into a mirror that reflects our daily routines and behaviors. These patterns, often unconscious, dictate how we spend our time and energy, influencing our productivity and personal development. To transform effectively, we need to evaluate our daily routines and recognize which behaviors support our goals and which don't. This process requires honesty and empathy towards ourselves as we meticulously observe our actions and their impact on our lives. By identifying these patterns, we lay the groundwork for meaningful change, giving ourselves the opportunity to redefine our days, align actions with values, and open the door to a life filled with purpose and intention.

Evaluating Existing Routines

Evaluating your existing routines is like holding up a mirror to your daily life. It's an exercise in self-awareness that can be both enlightening and, at times, challenging. Often, habits form without us even realizing it, subtly influencing our actions and choices. If you're seeking to transform your habits for enhanced productivity and personal growth, you've got to start by examining where you're currently standing. This requires courage and honesty, as it involves taking a good, hard look at what comprises your day-to-day behaviors.

Start by observing your daily patterns. What activities fill your day from morning to night? It might help to jot them down in a journal or use an app to track them. Focus not just on the "what" but also the "why." Why do you reach for your phone first thing in the morning? Why do you find yourself snacking in the afternoon? Recognizing these routines brings you a step closer to understanding the triggers that drive them.

Take note of the emotions tied to these habits. Sometimes routines are born out of necessity, sometimes out of comfort, and other times out of avoidance. Dissecting these emotions can shine a light on why certain routines have cemented their place in your life. And remember, it's not about labeling habits as good or bad but understanding their role in your life. What do they fulfill for you? What do they shield you from?

Your physical environment plays a crucial role as well. Examine how your surroundings support or deter your routines. Is your workspace cluttered? Does your living room invite lounging rather than activity? Such insights are pivotal because environments often reinforce habits without you even batting an eyelash.

An invaluable tool during this evaluation is feedback from those around you. They may recognize patterns you don't see, offering perspectives that illuminate blind spots. But it's key to remain open and not defensive; the goal is growth, not judgment. Seek out those who know you well and ask them about their observations. What changes have they noticed in your behavior over time?

You might uncover that certain habits fill unmet needs. Perhaps your nightly gaming session is a way to decompress, or maybe skipping breakfast isn't an oversight but a strategy to save time. Uncovering these nuances can guide you toward more effective habit modification strategies tailored to your unique circumstances.

Don't underestimate the impact of smaller, seemingly insignificant routines. They often build momentum over time, transforming into larger patterns that can help or hinder your growth. The habit of reading a page before bed could grow into a voracious reading appetite, or the tendency to leave tasks unfinished might snowball into chronic procrastination.

Identifying patterns is about connecting the dots of your daily life. It involves asking tough questions and being patient with yourself as you search for answers. Embrace this exploration as an opportunity to better understand who you are and what drives you, laying the groundwork for the changes you wish to make.

It's also crucial to recognize the routines that positively shape your life. These might be habits you've developed through effort or ones that emerged effortlessly. Celebrate them. Acknowledging your strengths can boost your confidence and serve as a foundation upon which to build new habits.

Change often begins with awareness. By the time you've critically evaluated your existing routines, you'll have a clearer picture of where you stand. This clarity can fuel your journey toward meaningful transformation, empowering you to design routines that truly reflect your goals and values.

Recognizing Detrimental Behaviors

Every person carries with them a set of behaviors that blaze a trail through their daily life. Yet, not all these behaviors propel us forward; some may tether us to patterns that impede growth. Recognizing detrimental behaviors is the initial step in unearthing the potential for personal evolution. It's an opportunity to transform habits that have served as talismans of stagnancy into catalysts for change.

Detrimental behaviors often seep into our lives subtly, masquerading as innocuous rituals or survival mechanisms. They may originate from unresolved past experiences or develop as responses to stress. These habits can manifest in various forms: procrastination, excessive screen time, negative self-talk, or unhealthy coping strategies. The commonality among them is their capacity to derange progress and curtail aspirations. By identifying these behaviors, we cast light on the shadows obfuscating our path to self-betterment.

Have you ever wondered why certain actions persist despite being counterproductive? It's because habits, once rooted, become automated. The mind, always in search of efficiency, relegates these patterns to subconscious processes, sparing us from constant deliberation. However, this automation is a double-edged sword—it conserves mental energy but also renders us prisoners of our routines. Recognizing detrimental behaviors requires a conscious effort to shine a spotlight on these mental shortcuts and challenge their necessity.

Taking stock of your current patterns entails a candid introspection. It's a process that asks: What am I doing that isn't serving me? This isn't about self-reproach but self-discovery. By understanding the behaviors that stifle us, we embark on the journey of change with a clear map of where the current road ends. This clarity is vital, for you can't change what you don't recognize.

One approach to bring these behaviors to the forefront is by keeping a behavior journal. Documenting your actions, emotions, and contexts in a non-judgmental manner can reveal the hidden triggers and patterns of detrimental habits. Patterns are elusive until they're pinned down in ink; only then do they lose their invisibility cloaks and reveal their true nature. By consistently journaling, you gather data that's crucial for understanding the 'why' behind persistent habits.

It's essential to approach this undertaking with compassion. Too often, the discovery of detrimental behaviors can lead to harsh self-criticism. But understanding these behaviors through the lens of empathy enables us to view them as remnants of past survival strategies rather than personal failings. Recognizing that everyone harbors some level of maladaptive behaviors allows us to connect with our humane sides and approach change with kindness.

Moreover, detrimental behaviors exist within a broader context of triggers and environments that facilitate their emergence. Social pressures, work demands, or even the very spaces we inhabit can foster these behaviors. Recognizing them means considering the constellation of conditions surrounding them. Are there specific interactions or settings that feed these habits? By identifying these contributory factors, the task of altering behavior becomes more manageable and less daunting.

In some instances, addressing these behaviors involves acknowledging their underlying pain. Unmet needs or unresolved emotions often lurk beneath the surface, driving habits that merely serve as coping mechanisms. Understanding this connection deepens the recognition process and opens the door to addressing root causes rather than merely symptoms. An empathetic exploration of these emotions can be both revelatory and healing, providing a solid foundation for sustainable change.

Empowerment in recognizing detrimental behaviors lies not only in identifying them but in choosing to forge a new path. This decision marks the beginning of redefining habits that align more harmoniously with your personal growth and well-being. Remember, every detrimental behavior once served a purpose, however misguided it now seems. By recognizing and reframing these patterns, you reclaim agency over your narrative and invite transformation.

The commitment to identifying and altering these behaviors is undeniably challenging but profoundly rewarding. It requires courage to confront the comfort of familiarity and venture into the realm of self-improvement. As you delve deeper into recognizing detrimental behaviors, embrace the journey as an adventure in self-discovery. Each revelation is a step closer to the life you envision, equipped with the knowledge that you possess the power to change.

Chapter 3: The Science of Change

In our journey of personal transformation, understanding the science of change acts as a guiding beacon. Behavioral change isn't just about willpower; it's about understanding how our brains work and how habits are formed and reformed. This chapter delves into the intricate mechanisms at play, where neuroscience and psychology merge to unravel the complexity of making lasting changes. By gaining insights into how our neural pathways adapt, we're empowered to craft strategies that stick, turning daunting challenges into manageable steps. It's the fusion of knowledge and action that ignites true transformation, giving us the tools to reshape our behaviors and, ultimately, our lives. Recognizing these principles frees us to pursue meaningful growth, knowing we've got the capability of change wired within us.

Behavior Modification Basics

Embarking on the journey of behavior modification is like unraveling the intricate layers of our daily routines and choices. It all starts with the realization that the patterns we live by, often unconsciously, shape who we are and ultimately determine our success in personal and professional realms. For many, the idea of changing these deep-seated behaviors might feel daunting. However, implementing simple yet effective strategies can transform these apparently rigid patterns into stepping stones toward growth and productivity.

At its core, behavior modification involves understanding the mechanisms that drive our habits. The power of behavior change comes from its simplicity: identifying a behavior, understanding its triggers, and systematically altering the responses and rewards associated with it. Behavioral psychology provides the foundation for this process, detailing how habits are formed and sustained. Central to this transformation is recognizing the "cue-routine-reward" loop—a cycle that perpetuates habits, both good and bad. To break free or build anew, we must first dissect this loop.

Changing behavior is not about immediate, drastic overhauls. It is a gradual process that begins with small, intentional steps. The first step in altering any behavior is self-awareness. Taking a closer look at our habits, without judgment, allows us to identify which ones aid in our growth and which serve as barriers. Reflection can spark the motivation needed for change, as it offers clarity about why we behave the way we do.

Once we're aware of these patterns, the next challenge is replacing detrimental routines with beneficial ones. This is often where people stumble, as change can be uncomfortable. Success lies in the small wins—incremental changes that accumulate over time to create significant transformation. By focusing on one behavior at a time and substituting it with a new, healthier routine, we set ourselves up for long-term success. For instance, replacing the habit of reaching for a sugary snack when stressed with a few minutes of deep breathing or a short walk can gradually modulate the body's stress response.

The environment in which we operate plays a critical role in behavior modification. By creating supportive surroundings, we can reinforce positive behaviors and minimize negative cues. This could involve simple changes like placing a book beside your coffee mug to encourage morning reading or setting reminders to take standing breaks throughout the day. Our environment should be structured to assist us in making the right choices effortlessly.

Meanwhile, accountability acts as a powerful catalyst for change. Sharing your goals with someone trustworthy can provide support and encouragement when motivation wanes. It's the shared journey, the collective accountability, that can often make the process of behavior modification less solitary and more connected. By doing so, not only do we keep ourselves in check, but we also cultivate a network of encouragement and reinforcement.

Motivation is another essential component in modifying behaviors. It fuels the persistence needed to change and sustain new habits. Understanding one's intrinsic motivations—

those deep internal reasons for change—ensures longevity in behavioral shifts. It's crucial to ask ourselves why we want to change and what outcomes we hope to achieve. This intrinsic drive must be nurtured and revisited, especially when faced with obstacles.

Additionally, it's essential to recognize that behavior modification is rarely linear. It's filled with potential setbacks and deviations from the intended path. This understanding helps in building resilience and fostering a growth mindset. Resilience allows us to view setbacks not as failures, but as feedback and opportunities for learning. Adjustments along the journey are not only expected but are vital in crafting a personalized path that aligns with individual values and goals.

Finally, it's important to celebrate successes—both big and small. Recognizing and rewarding ourselves for progress, no matter how minor it may seem, reinforces the behaviors and increases the likelihood of their repetition. Consistency, over time, breeds mastery. By nurturing new behaviors with patience and perseverance, they become ingrained as natural extensions of our identity.

Behavior modification is indeed a journey, and every step forward is a testament to our capability for change and adaptation. With intention, the right strategies, and a supportive environment, the habits that once seemed immovable can transform into foundations for a fulfilled, productive life.

The Neurology Behind Habit Changes

Change is a marvel of the human experience, as intricate and complex as the brain itself. Our ability to modify our habits is rooted deeply in the neural pathways that form through consistent behavior. At its core, changing a habit is more than just a matter of willpower—it's a neurological transformation. Understanding this transformation can empower us to master our habits and enhance personal growth. It's not magic; it's science.

Our brains thrive on efficiency, which is why habits exist. They allow us to perform everyday activities without a constant need for conscious thought, reserving our mental capacity for more complex tasks. This efficiency is achieved through the basal ganglia, a group of nuclei in the brain involved in movement and emotions, where habitual patterns are cemented. When we initiate a habit, it begins in the prefrontal cortex, the area responsible for decision-making and self-control. However, as the habit becomes ingrained, control shifts to the basal ganglia, freeing up the prefrontal cortex for other tasks.

The process of habituation involves three stages: the cue, the routine, and the reward. As you might already know, these elements form the habit loop, a concept popularized in recent discussions of neuroscience and behavioral science. The cue triggers the routine, which is the behavior itself, and the reward reinforces this loop, solidifying the habit in your neural circuitry. The brain craves this reward, which is why breaking a habit or forming a new one isn't about resisting temptation—it's about reconfiguring this loop.

Let's dig a little deeper. When you embark on changing a habit, it's essential to understand neuroplasticity—the brain's capability to reorganize itself by forming new neural connections. This ability is at the heart of habit change. Although this plasticity is more pronounced in children, adults too possess significant capacity for brain reorganization. Making a conscious effort to alter your habits leverages this inherent adaptability.

Consider the metaphor of a well-trodden path in a forest. Habits carve similar paths in your brain, simplifying every step you take. To change a habit, you must pave a new path, which can initially seem challenging and slow-moving. However, each repetition strengthens this new path, eventually turning it into the dominant route, while the former path fades away. This process elucidates why persistence and patience are vital when cultivating new habits.

Indeed, breaking bad habits is often more difficult than forming new ones because they are firmly entrenched routes in our neural landscape. The prefrontal cortex must remain engaged to suppress the old habit, making the process cognitively taxing. However, the science of habit change offers a silver lining: replacing an old habit with a new one is usually more effective than attempting mere elimination.

The chemical aspect of our brains also plays a significant role in habit formation and change. Neurotransmitters such as dopamine are crucial in regulating our pleasure and reward pathways, actively reinforcing habitual behaviors. The release of dopamine following a habitual action not only rewards the brain but compels it to seek that reward repeatedly. Hence, understanding how to manipulate these reward systems can aid in effectively reorienting habits. Associating new, healthier habits with rewarding stimuli helps in reshaping behavioral patterns more enjoyably and sustainably.

As we dig deeper into the intricacies of neurons and synapses, it's also important to acknowledge the emotional layers involved in habit change. Emotional triggers can often dictate the success or failure of altering these deep-seated patterns. Emotional intelligence, therefore, becomes a valuable ally when navigating this complex territory. Cultivating self-awareness helps in identifying emotional cues that can reinforce or disrupt habit loops.

Empathy, towards oneself, acts as a potent catalyst in this scenario. Recognizing that falling back into old habits occasionally is part of the journey can foster resilience, creating a space for growth without self-punishment. This perspective shifts the focus from perfection to progress, nurturing a growth mindset that aligns with sustained habit transformation.

The relationship between habits and the brain's reward system implies that something as subtle as changing the context of a cue or gradually modifying a routine can eventually transform a habit loop. Take, for instance, the habit of late-night snacking driven by stress. By identifying the trigger (stress), you can begin to reshape the pathway by substituting the routine with a relaxing activity like reading or meditation. The new habit may not bring immediate satisfaction, but with time, patience, and reinforcement, it can parallel the satisfaction once provided by snacking.

Importantly, the collaborative support of our communities and environments can significantly bolster these neurological endeavors. The mirrored neurons in our brains react to the behaviors of others around us. Therefore, surrounding oneself with individuals who embody desired habits can promote those behaviors in our own lives. The brain adapts, influenced not only internally but by the external social stimuli it often mirrors.

In closing, understanding the neurology behind habit changes equips us with the knowledge to take control of our behaviors. It reminds us that change is not only possible; it's within reach. By appreciating the brain's capacity for adaptation and harnessing the power of neuroplasticity, we can effectively reshape our lives, step by motivational step. Yes, the path to change is layered with complexity, but with the brain as our guide, we're not merely rewriting patterns. We're sculpting a new, dynamic version of ourselves ready to seize opportunities for growth and productivity.

Chapter 4: Building New Routines

As we transition from understanding and identifying our existing patterns, it's time to focus on creating routines that lead to personal growth and improved productivity. Building new routines is like crafting a blueprint for your future, where each deliberate action contributes to a more fulfilling life. The key lies in recognizing the potency of small, consistent steps that, over time, form the foundation of transformative change. Embracing this process requires not just an understanding of what habits you want but a commitment to nurturing them with intention. This is where the magic happens—by setting up beneficial habits aligned with your goals, you create a resilient framework for success. Rather than overwhelming yourself with massive changes, ditch the all-or-nothing mindset and celebrate the incremental victories. Every choice becomes a building block, and with persistence and patience, the seemingly mundane efforts will culminate in extraordinary results. By taking a proactive approach, you empower yourself to reshape your daily life, making each day an opportunity to grow closer to the person you've always aspired to become.

Setting Up Beneficial Habits

Setting up beneficial habits is often seen as the foundation of a fulfilling life. It's the launching pad from which personal growth and productivity take flight. But how do we plant these seeds that flourish into routines supporting our ambitions? The answer lies in understanding the dynamics of habit formation and intentionally crafting our daily practices.

At its core, setting up a new habit involves a vision of what you wish to achieve. Begin with clarity. Imagine the end result, whether it's waking up early, exercising regularly, or setting aside daily reading time. Visualizing the purpose of your intended habit instills a sense of direction. It's the 'why' that fuels the persistence needed to see it through challenging phases. Crafting this vision is less about seeking perfection and more about discovering a meaningful goal that resonates with your values.

Once you've identified the desired habit, the next step is to create a plan. Start small—aim for incremental changes rather than a complete overhaul. The power of small steps cannot be overstated. A tiny adjustment to your routine, like setting out your workout clothes the night before an exercise session, can become a powerful cue that sets the cycle of habit formation in motion. It's these cues, inserted thoughtfully into your daily routine, that help habits latch onto your subconscious.

Don't underestimate the role of consistency in nurturing new habits. Repetition solidifies the neural pathways associated with a particular behavior, transforming it from a conscious effort to an automatic response. Establishing a consistent routine demands commitment, yet it's in these repeated actions that habits take root. Like tending to a garden, daily cultivation produces the most vibrant blooms.

Moreover, it's essential to engineer your environment to support your budding habits. If you're aiming to eat healthier, stock your kitchen with nutritious options. If you want to delve into mindfulness, create a serene space in your home dedicated to meditation. Your environment should echo your objectives, subtly nudging you toward fulfilling your new habits without conscious effort.

Enlisting support from your social circle can propel your habit-forming journey. Share your goals with a trusted friend or join a community with similar aspirations. The backing of others provides accountability and encouragement. It showcases the ripple effect of habits, where one person's positive change inspires another, creating a supportive network that amplifies your efforts.

To remain motivated, recognize and celebrate small victories along the way. Every time you brush against a milestone, no matter how minor, take a moment to acknowledge your achievement. Progress is addictive—each accomplishment fuels your desire for further success, making the journey both rewarding and motivational.

What if a new habit doesn't fit, or resistance emerges? Adaptability is key. Don't hesitate to tweak or pivot your approach. Flexibility allows you to navigate obstacles and maintain momentum. It's normal for new habits to feel awkward or forced initially. Over time, as they align more naturally with your lifestyle, their benefits will outweigh any early discomforts.

Every so often, evaluate the effectiveness of your habits. Are they still in alignment with your overarching goals? Are they providing the outcomes you envisioned? Self-reflection ensures that your efforts contribute positively to your life and don't veer off course. If adjustments are needed, make them with confidence and maintain faith in the process.

Remember, transformation is a journey, not a destination. It's about the evolution of your routines into forces for positive change. As you cultivate beneficial habits, you're essentially rewriting the narrative of your life. Every day is an opportunity to choose a path that empowers you, to walk in the direction of your dreams, and to etch new patterns into your story.

The Power of Small Steps

One of the most compelling strategies in the journey of personal development and productivity is the concept of small steps. It's easy to overlook their significance, especially when aiming for transformation. But, these seemingly insignificant actions hold immense potential. They're like seeds, planting the foundation for robust, enduring changes over time.

Consider the analogy of building a wall. Every brick laid, on its own, might seem inconsequential, but together, they form a solid structure. Similarly, small actions might not offer immediate results, but collectively, they create the foundation for powerful habits. The journey of creating change often begins with these tiny steps, steps that set off a ripple effect leading to deeper, more substantial progress.

So why do small steps work? It's because they bypass our brain's resistance to change. When faced with a daunting task, our natural reaction can be to back away. However, small steps gently invite us to engage without overwhelming us. They require minimal willpower, yet they keep us moving forward, amalgamating into an unstoppable momentum over time.

One effective method to embrace small steps is the "two-minute rule," which suggests starting a new habit by dedicating just two minutes to it. This technique relies on the concept that initiating a task is often the most challenging part. Once we start, we're more likely to keep going, and by consistently applying this rule, new habits can seamlessly integrate into our routines.

Consistency is the unsung hero in personal development. It's not about the size of the step but the frequency of taking actions. Consistent small actions not only contribute incrementally to greater achievements but also reinforce our self-efficacy. Each completed small task is like a vote of confidence in ourselves, a reminder that we are capable of change.

However, the magic of small steps doesn't just lie in their ability to breach our mental barriers. They also allow for real-time feedback and adjustments. Because the stakes are lower, we can afford to experiment, learn, and recalibrate without much risk. This iterative process can be highly beneficial for anyone looking to fine-tune their approach to building new routines.

Creating deliberate pauses to evaluate these small steps can propel progress even further. It's during these moments that we reflect on what worked, what didn't, and what could be adjusted. This reflection ensures that our small steps are not just routine drudgery but purposeful actions aligned with our larger goals.

Furthermore, the psychological impact of completing these small steps can't be underestimated. Each small victory releases a dose of dopamine in our brain, which signals pleasure and satisfaction. These feelings of reward keep us motivated, enhancing our commitment to pursuing the habit even when the initial excitement wanes.

Take, for instance, the habit of reading. Breaking it down, you could start with reading one page a day. It sounds trivial but think about what happens after a month or a year. The accumulation of small daily practices leads to significant knowledge and fosters a love for learning.

The beauty of small steps is that they democratize progress. Everyone, regardless of current skill level or past experiences, can take a small step. It's about finding that initial spark of action that feels manageable. For someone starting a fitness journey, a small step could be taking a five-minute walk. For another, it might be writing a single paragraph for a potential novel.

Yet, while small steps are vital, it's important to maintain a broader vision. Small steps should seamlessly fit within a grander blueprint of your aspirations. These minor actions need direction and purpose, which come from a clearly defined goal. The harmony between small steps and an overarching vision ensures that daily actions lead towards meaningful outcomes.

With time, the power of these small steps can be transformative. As they build upon one another, they grow into habits and routines that not only support personal growth but also redefine who we are. They cultivate discipline, patience, and resilience—traits necessary for any personal development journey. Over time, what starts as a mere experiment with small steps becomes a profound exploration into deep-seated capabilities.

Celebrate these small steps. Even when they feel baby in comparison to the giants of your ambitions, know that they are paving the way to progress. Acknowledge their power, applaud the subtle yet sure changes they incite, and let them guide you to your ultimate goals.

The journey of personal transformation is not about radical leaps. It's about the gradual evolution shaped by small, deliberate steps. They demonstrate that we don't have to do everything at once, and by embracing this philosophy, we encourage ourselves to stay committed, persistent, and remain hopeful in the face of challenges.

Chapter 5: Overcoming Resistance

As we delve into the concept of overcoming resistance, it's crucial to acknowledge that this journey involves facing a formidable internal adversary that often lurks in the shadows of our ambitions and intentions: self-doubt. This resistance is a subtle yet powerful force, attempting to anchor us in our comfort zones, whispering fears of inadequacy and failure. Yet, it's in the moment we recognize resistance not as a barrier, but as an opportunity for growth, that we begin to harness the courage to push through. Strategies for overcoming this resistance require a blend of self-awareness and resilience, calling upon us to challenge limiting beliefs and redefine what success looks like. Motivation wanes and waxes, but understanding the root causes of resistance, whether they're rooted in fear or habit, empowers us to persevere. It's about cultivating a mindset that doesn't just endure challenges but embraces them as steps toward becoming the person you've envisioned. Through the trials of resistance, we'll find a path to not only new habits but a deeper, more profound personal development.

Tackling Internal Obstacles

Change doesn't always come easy. If there's one truth about seeking personal growth through habit transformation, it's that our biggest hurdles often lie within ourselves. Internal obstacles, those psychological barriers and deep-seated fears, can seem daunting. But understanding them is the first step toward moving past them.

At the heart of every internal obstacle is fear. We fear change, not just because it's unfamiliar, but also because it challenges the very essence of who we are. This fear can manifest as self-doubt, insecurity, and even procrastination. To tackle these obstacles head-on, we must first recognize and acknowledge them without judgment. It's important to understand that fear is a natural part of the growth process.

Once you identify these fears, examine the stories you're telling yourself. Are you convincing yourself that change is impossible? Do you believe that failure is inevitable? Such narratives often stem from past experiences or deep-seated beliefs that no longer serve you. By questioning their validity, you start dismantling their power over you.

Self-awareness is a critical tool in this process. It involves being mindful of your thoughts and emotions as they arise. When temptations to revert to old habits emerge, pause, and ask yourself why. Is there an underlying discomfort or anxiety you're avoiding? Taking time to reflect and journal about these experiences can enhance your understanding and lead to breakthroughs.

Moreover, consider the impact of *self-compassion*. We are often our harshest critics, punishing ourselves for every perceived flaw or setback. Practicing self-compassion means treating yourself with the same kindness and understanding that you would offer a friend. It means accepting that mistakes are part of learning and growth. By doing so, you disarm the fear of failure, transforming it into a learning opportunity.

Visualizing success is another potent strategy. Picture yourself confidently adopting new habits and reaping the benefits they bring. Visualization helps to create a mental image of success, making it feel more attainable and reinforcing your motivation to overcome internal challenges.

Yet, visualization alone isn't enough. **Taking action** is essential. Start with small, incremental steps that gradually build toward your goals. This approach not only makes change less intimidating but also helps establish a pattern of success. As you experience victories, no matter how minor, your confidence grows, further weakening the internal barriers you face.

A practical action plan might include setting specific, achievable goals, monitoring your progress, and celebrating small wins. This structured approach provides clarity and purpose, reducing the chaos that often accompanies behavior change. Remember, consistency is key. It's not about being perfect every day but about continuing to move forward, even if that progress seems small.

Another crucial aspect is to cultivate a supportive inner dialogue. Replace self-criticism with affirmations and supportive messages. When self-doubt tries to take hold, remind yourself of your capabilities and progress. Over time, this positive reinforcement can shift your mindset, making it easier to push through resistance.

Additionally, forgiveness plays a vital role in overcoming internal obstacles. We must be willing to forgive ourselves when we struggle or falter. Holding onto guilt or regret only fans the flames of self-doubt, making it harder to move forward. Forgiving yourself allows you to let go of the past and focus on the present, where change is possible.

Consider involving trusted friends or mentors in your journey. Sharing your challenges with someone who understands and supports your goals can alleviate some of the burdens of change. They can offer encouragement, advice, and accountability, helping you stay on track when internal doubts threaten to derail your efforts.

Lastly, patience is a virtue you can't overlook. Habit transformation isn't an overnight endeavor. Be patient with yourself as you navigate new terrain and face setbacks. Progress might be slower than you'd like, but every step forward, no matter how small, is valuable.

In tackling these internal challenges, remember that you're engaging in a deeply personal journey. It's about growth and self-discovery as much as it's about habit change. Embrace this journey with an open heart and mind. In doing so, you're not just overcoming resistance; you're building a resilient mindset that will serve you well in all areas of life.

As we move forward in transforming our habits, encouraging words become a source of strength. They remind us that internal obstacles, though formidable, are surmountable. Within the heart of struggle lies potential, waiting to be unleashed through perseverance and courage.

Strategies for Sustained Motivation

Overcoming resistance is undoubtedly a formidable challenge in the journey of transforming one's habits. To break through these barriers and foster lasting change, strategic approaches to sustaining motivation are required. Motivation is not a static entity; it's a dynamic force that ebbs and flows, influenced by our circumstances, emotions, and environment. But what truly distinguishes those who succeed in personal development from those who falter is not the absence of setbacks, but rather the resilience to return, re-evaluate, and reignite their motivation.

One effective strategy for maintaining motivation is to connect deeply with your personal "why." It's crucial to identify the underlying reasons why you want to change a habit. Is it to improve your health, enhance your productivity, or perhaps achieve a long-held aspiration? When you have a clear and compelling reason, that sense of purpose can serve as an anchor during times of wavering commitment. By keeping your focus on the bigger picture, you strengthen the motivation muscle required to overcome any instances of resistance.

Another potent strategy is to set specific, achievable goals. Vague objectives can lead to indecision and decrease motivation. Instead, break your big goals into smaller, manageable milestones. As each milestone is achieved, it triggers a sense of accomplishment, reinforcing your desire to continue. This approach isn't merely about checking off tasks; it's about building positive momentum. Celebrating small wins can boost your motivation significantly, acting as a reminder of the progress you're making, however incremental.

Social accountability is a powerful motivator. Sharing your goals with friends, a supportive community, or even a mentor can create a network of encouragement and accountability. When others are aware of your objectives, the psychological need not to let them down can bolster your resolve to pursue them. Additionally, engaging with others on similar paths can create opportunities for shared learning and mutual encouragement, further strengthening the bonds that keep you moving forward.

Regular reflection is essential to sustained motivation. Taking time to reflect on your journey provides clarity on what's working and what isn't. Reflection doesn't merely involve looking back; it also entails adjusting for the future. By regularly assessing your progress, setbacks can be addressed proactively rather than reactively. This adaptive approach keeps motivation fresh and relevant, reducing the psychological toll of perceived failure.

Intrinsic motivation, or the drive that comes from within, is more sustainable than relying solely on extrinsic rewards. Finding joy in the process itself can be incredibly rewarding. Whether it's the quiet satisfaction of completing a workout, the intellectual stimulation from reading, or the peacefulness of a tidy workspace, these internal rewards can be more effective in the long run. When you learn to love the process, not just the outcome, motivation becomes a more consistent ally.

Visual reminders of your goals can serve as powerful motivators. Vision boards, journal entries, or a simple sticky note on your bathroom mirror can remind you of your ultimate objectives and the reasons behind them. These visual cues act as constant reminders to keep moving forward, reinforcing your commitment every time you see them. The continual reinforcement ensures that your goals remain at the forefront of your daily activities, sustaining your motivation.

Developing resilience is another critical strategy for maintaining motivation. Resilience enables you to weather the inevitable ups and downs on the path to change. It encompasses acceptance of the fact that not every day will be perfect; setbacks are part of the journey. Resilient individuals learn from their mistakes instead of being thwarted by them. They hone the ability to quickly recover, adapt, and drive forward with renewed vigor.

Identifying and mitigating the barriers that challenge your motivation can be transformative. These barriers can be emotional, such as fear and self-doubt, or practical, like time management and resource availability. Tackling these head-on through strategic planning allows you to create a more favorable environment for maintaining motivation. Whether it involves setting boundaries, seeking professional guidance, or reorganizing your schedule, these efforts pay substantial dividends.

Incorporating mindfulness practices can also aid in maintaining motivation. Mindfulness encourages living in the present, acknowledging feelings and thoughts without judgment. This awareness increases your capacity to understand what truly motivates you, aiding in aligning your everyday actions with your inner values. It reduces stress and helps maintain clear focus, thereby fostering a fertile ground for motivation.

The journey of habit change is unique for everyone, reflecting individual challenges and contexts. To sustain motivation over the long term, flexibility in your approach is paramount. As life circumstances change, so too should your strategies for motivation. Adopting a mindset open to adaptation ensures that motivational tools stay relevant and effective regardless of the changing landscape of your personal and professional life.

Finally, it's essential to embrace the inevitability of change. Understand that motivation may wax and wane, but with the right strategies in place, it can always be reignited. Constant vigilance over your motivation levels and proactive strategies can make the difference between stagnation and continual personal growth. Equip yourself with these approaches, and you'll find that overcoming resistance becomes not only achievable but an integral part of your journey towards habit mastery.

Chapter 6: Harnessing Habits for Productivity

As we turn our attention to using habits to supercharge our productivity, it becomes clear that the secret lies in blending discipline with daily life. Habits can be seen as the autopilot of our actions, directing much of what we do without conscious effort. Establishing purposeful routines is integral to productivity, as they allow us to focus our mental energy on tasks that require creativity and problem-solving, rather than repetitive decisions. Integrating techniques like chunking tasks into manageable parts or using time-blocking methods can transform our routines into powerhouses of efficiency. By making deliberate choices about where our habits lead us, we not only prioritize what truly matters but also create a stable structure that supports our ambitions. Harnessing this potential requires both introspection and commitment, but the payoff is a sense of flow in our daily endeavors, where progress feels seamless and personal growth is constantly within reach.

Techniques for Improved Efficiency

Improving efficiency through habits can feel like unraveling a personal mystery, where each clue leads to a more productive and fulfilling life. Habits form the backbone of our daily routines, but when tailored properly, they can drive efficiency to new heights. It's about rewiring patterns so they not only coincide with productivity but also resonate with your personal goals and values. To begin this transformation, it's imperative to delve into techniques that heighten your efficiency without sacrificing your well-being or personal interests.

One potent technique involves *task batching*. By grouping similar tasks, you reduce the mental load and transition time between diverse activities. For instance, setting aside a specific time to respond to emails rather than repeatedly throughout the day can improve workflow and creativity. Task batching allows you to stay in the same mental zone, cutting down on the time and energy it takes to switch contexts. Not to mention, it frees up mental space for more demanding or high-priority projects.

Closely related is **time blocking**, a strategy where you divide your day into blocks dedicated to specific activities. Instead of a chaotic to-do list, you use your calendar as a dynamic planner, allocating specific hours to focus on particular tasks. This not only helps in completing activities within strict timeframes but also brings clarity and discipline to your day. Time blocking demands you to identify priority tasks, ensuring that time magnifies what matters most. It also makes it easier to keep track of balance between work, rest, and leisure, essential elements for sustainable efficiency.

Integrating automation where possible can dramatically uplift efficiency. Automation isn't limited to technological tasks; it can involve creating routines that minimize decision-making. Designing morning rituals or default evening routines can curtail decision fatigue, leaving more acumen for complex challenges. Moreover, employing digital tools that manage reminders, payments, or even grocery shopping can recapture time that's better spent elsewhere. By offloading these repetitive processes, you free mental bandwidth for creative and strategic thinking.

Sometimes, improving efficiency necessitates saying "no." It's difficult, especially when you want to be everything to everyone. Yet, the art of strategic refusal can foster more focused efforts on the commitments that truly propel you forward. Having the clarity and courage to decline tasks that don't align with your goals ensures energy isn't wasted on non-contributory activities. It's about embracing the selective mindset and judiciously choosing where you invest time and energy.

Feedback loops are equally valuable. They provide insights not only into your progress but also where adjustments are necessary. Employing regular reflection, whether daily or weekly, allows you to assess what's working and what's diverting you from your objectives. Such analysis sharpens your understanding and ability to tweak habits when required, ensuring continuous improvement in your journey for enhanced productivity.

Your environment significantly impacts your efficiency. Creating a workspace that inspires you yet minimizes distractions is crucial. Think of a dedicated and organized space that encourages focus, whether it's a tidy home office or a simple, clutter-free corner. This environment isn't just physical but also digital. Managing digital notifications, having a clear email inbox, or organizing digital files aids in keeping your virtual space conducive to productivity. A well-curated environment supports your routine, reducing the friction between you and your work.

Understanding the rhythms of your body and mind leads to the exploitation of *peak productivity windows*. Each person has unique cycles where focus, energy, and creativity reach their zenith. Identify these periods to allocate the most challenging tasks when you're operating at your best. Conversely, use low-energy times for less demanding or routine tasks like administrative work. Effectively synchronizing your activities with your natural ebbs and flows means requires less effort for optimal output.

Incorporate **mindfulness practices** that keep stress at bay and enhance concentration. Short meditation sessions, breathing exercises, or even mindful walking breaks can refuel your mind, lowering stress and raising your efficiency. Mindfulness isn't about secluding yourself from the world but learning to be present, improving your ability to focus on tasks at hand while maintaining an overall sense of calm. The quieter mind navigates the complexities of work and life with ease, unlocking a straightforward path to productivity.

Establishing an accountability system provides an additional layer of commitment to your goals. Whether you're sharing intentions with a colleague, using an app, or joining a focused group, this external support can reinforce motivation and discipline. Regular check-ins with accountability partners can highlight progress, illuminate areas for improvement, and even spark new ideas. The external perspective can confirm that your actions are aligned with your ambitions, keeping you grounded and on track.

Ultimately, these techniques equip you with a robust toolkit for boosting productivity through habit refinement. Efficiency isn't just about getting more done—it's about doing things better and more consciously. By harnessing your habits, you transform them into stepping stones that lead not just to efficiency, but also to fulfillment and personal development. Remember, consistent small improvements culminate in monumental transformations, and this collection of strategies is your compass on the quest toward an optimized, productive life.

Prioritizing Tasks Through Routine

Routines can be incredibly powerful, allowing us to seamlessly integrate tasks and cultivate habits that enhance our productivity in profound ways. The core of harnessing routines lies not just in repetition but in prioritization. When you learn how to prioritize tasks through a well-crafted routine, you essentially give structure to potential chaos. Instead of letting the overwhelming number of tasks determine your day, you take charge by deciding what truly matters and when. A purposefully designed routine prevents inconsequential tasks from cluttering your to-do list, ensuring that your focus remains on what truly drives value and fulfillment.

First, let's talk about the inevitability of tasks. Our lives are filled with a mix of vital responsibilities and mundane chores. Imagine a routine as the spine of your day, holding everything together with coherent strength. But a spine can't support every burden equally — it needs precise placement of priorities to prevent collapse. By identifying what tasks align with your core goals and values, you create a hierarchical system where the compelling purpose becomes the guiding light of your routine. This alignment shadows each task, whether small or complex, with meaning.

To effectively prioritize tasks, start by distinguishing between urgent and important activities. This concept, often discussed in productivity circles, emphasizes that not everything urgent is important, and not everything important is urgent. A task's urgency might require immediate attention, but importance is derived from its long-term impact on your goals. When establishing your routine, allocate slots for tasks based on their significance rather than their noise. Integrating this mindset into your routines ensures that you focus on tasks that bring you closer to your aspirations, rather than getting caught in the allure of immediate, albeit superficial, accomplishments.

Moreover, routines act as a buffer against decision fatigue. Every day, we're faced with a barrage of choices, and the process of deciding can become a significant drain on our mental energy. By integrating prioritization into your routine, you reduce the number of decisions you need to make. A well-set routine pre-decides what needs attention, so you don't have to deliberate each action anew each day. This simplicity not only saves time but also preserves your mental faculties for tasks that genuinely require your cognitive focus.

Consider the role of time-blocking as a practical tool for prioritizing within your routines. Time-blocking involves allocating specific time slots for different activities. This aligns your tasks with your energy levels throughout the day, maximizing efficiency. For instance, if you perform analytical work better in the morning, reserve those hours for challenging tasks. Similarly, use low-energy periods for routine work or for brainstorming creative ideas, thus optimizing your capabilities in accordance with the time of day.

But setting priorities isn't a one-time action; it's a dynamic process. As circumstances change, so too should your priorities and routines. Regularly evaluating and reflecting on your routines ensures they remain aligned with your evolving goals and environment. The reality is, a routine that worked beautifully last month may no longer serve you as effectively today. Flexibility is crucial — it allows for adjustments and innovation, ensuring that your routine continues to propel you forward. To cement this adaptability, empower yourself with the practice of periodic routine audits, adjusting priorities as necessary to keep your productivity on track.

Another significant element of creating effective routines is the understanding of your optimal productivity windows. Each person has distinct periods during the day when they're naturally more alert and efficient. Recognizing and harnessing these windows by scheduling the highest priority tasks during these times can significantly enhance productivity. Communicating with your internal clock not only makes prioritization feasible but also organically aligns your body's rhythm with your daily responsibilities.

Prioritization through routines also involves setting boundaries. Saying 'no' is an often undervalued skill in maintaining focus on your priorities. While it might be tempting to accommodate requests and opportunities that come your way, discerning what aligns with your current goals is vital. Create a routine that definitively slots personal projects and pursuits, ensuring they don't get pushed aside by external demands. Reaffirming your priorities through these boundaries guards your time against dilution, keeping the essence of your goals intact.

Remember to integrate rest and reflection as part of your prioritized routine. It's easy to fill every moment with activities, but true productivity arises from balance. Allocating time for breaks and introspection ensures that you're not just moving forward blindly, but doing so with clarity and renewed intention. A routine that prunes your daily experience must also nurture, providing room for mental and emotional recuperation. This balance fosters a holistic approach to productivity, ensuring your journey is sustainable over the long haul.

Ultimately, prioritizing tasks through routine is about creating a harmonized dance between ambition and execution. It's about constructing a purposeful daily flow that doesn't just propel you through tasks but anchors each moment to your overarching vision. By prioritizing effectively, you transform your routine into a sanctuary of intent, where each action becomes a stepping stone towards meaningful achievement.

Chapter 7: Mastering Personal Growth

To truly master personal growth, one must embark on a profound journey of self-reflection and intentional action, aligning everyday habits with personal aspirations and values. It begins with a candid exploration of one's beliefs and the cultivation of a growth mindset, embracing the belief that abilities and intelligence can develop with effort and perseverance. This mindset fuels a transformative process where challenges are seen not as insurmountable obstacles but as opportunities for learning and development. As you align your habits with your goals, imagine each small step as a building block for your desired future, shaping not only daily routines but also the very essence of who you strive to become. With this alignment, your energy and focus manifest more effectively, fostering a life of purpose and fulfillment. By committing to this adaptive path, personal growth becomes a continuous, ever-evolving journey where each day presents a new opportunity to thrive beyond previous limitations.

Developing a Growth Mindset

When you're on a journey of personal growth, developing a growth mindset stands as a pivotal milestone. This mindset is often the difference between stalling and soaring, between dreams deferred and potential realized. Carol Dweck, a renowned psychologist, defines it as believing that abilities and intelligence can be developed through dedication and hard work. While the idea may seem simple, its impact is profound. Adopting a growth mindset doesn't just open doors to new possibilities; it changes the way you approach challenges, failures, and successes.

One of the hallmark characteristics of a growth mindset is the acceptance of challenges. Individuals who embrace this mindset see challenges as opportunities. They recognize that hardships aren't roadblocks but stepping stones to mastery. In contrast, a fixed mindset person might shy away from challenges, fearing failure or imperfection. The difference comes down to perception: do you see failure as detrimental, or as a chance to learn and adapt? This subtle shift in view can drastically alter your trajectory in personal development.

It's easy to view challenges as mountains too high to climb, but those with a growth mindset relish the climb itself. They're not solely focused on the summit; they're invested in the lessons learned and skills gained along the way. This approach builds resilience—a crucial ally when fostering personal growth. Resilience transforms setbacks into setups for comebacks, and with each comeback, you're emboldened, learning to handle future obstacles with confidence and grace. The journey itself becomes a valuable teacher.

Feedback plays a vital role in nurturing a growth mindset. Constructive criticism isn't something to shy away from—it's a tool to refine and improve your skills. Whether it's a colleague suggesting an alternate method or an internal realization about areas needing improvement, feedback becomes an integral part of your growth strategy. Instead of taking feedback as a personal affront, those with a growth mindset see it as data, feedback that can be analyzed, processed, and acted upon for better results.

Importantly, a growth mindset fosters a deep-seated belief in one's capability for change. Change is often daunting, especially when it involves altering ingrained habits and long-held beliefs. Yet, within the realm of personal growth, change is the only constant. It's essential to understand that effort and perseverance are the vehicles of change. With a growth mindset, you come to view effort not as fruitless toil but as a necessary investment to reap future rewards.

Consider the power of yet. Those with a growth mindset understand that just because they haven't mastered a skill yet doesn't mean they won't. The 'yet' is a powerhouse of potential, a silent reminder that capability evolves. "I can't do this" becomes "I can't do this yet," signifying an ongoing journey rather than a permanent state. Acknowledging this potential keeps the flame of motivation alive, even in the face of apparent failure.

Another crucial aspect of developing a growth mindset is self-compassion. Personal growth isn't about ruthless self-evaluation—it's about gentle yet firm encouragement. Mistakes are a natural part of any journey, and how you react to them speaks volumes. Instead of harsh self-criticism, those with a growth mindset practice self-kindness, understanding that mastery involves patience and persistence. This mindset fosters an environment where growth can thrive unencumbered by the fear of inadequacy.

Moreover, ambition is reframed within a growth mindset. It's not just a quest for success, but a passion for progress. The notion of 'success' is redefined to include the richness of the learning experience, not just the achievement of goals. This broader view unlocks endless potential, sidelining narrow definitions of success that can stifle creativity and innovation. By enjoying the process and not just the outcome, personal growth becomes a rewarding journey.

Cultivating a growth mindset involves surrounding yourself with supportive influences. Encouragement from friends, mentors, or even inspiring stories can reinforce your commitment to growth. These influences act as reminders that growth is a collective effort, and while the journey is uniquely personal, support can come from external sources too.

Another integral element of fostering a growth mindset is the celebration of others' successes. A growth mindset views another person's success as a source of inspiration, not jealousy. Celebrating others' accomplishments creates a vibrant environment where everyone can thrive, reinforcing that abundance is not limited but shared.

Finally, remember that developing a growth mindset is a journey in itself. It's not an overnight transformation but a continual process of introspection and adaptation. With practice, the neural pathways in your brain evolve, solidifying new patterns of thinking. Over time, you'll find that the challenges once feared become welcomed learning opportunities. Personal growth, therefore, becomes not just a destination but an exhilarating ongoing journey.

Embracing a growth mindset is embracing possibility, learning, and transformation. It's a commitment to self-improvement and a declaration that your potential is limitless. As you continue on your path to mastering personal growth, remember that the journey is just as significant as the destination. Each step forward is a testament to your dedication, showing that growth isn't just a goal—it's a way of life.

Aligning Habits with Personal Goals

In the journey of mastering personal growth, aligning habits with personal goals stands as a pivotal point of transition and transformation. This alignment doesn't happen accidentally; it requires intentional examination and decision-making. Habits, by nature, often go unnoticed as they are woven into the fabric of daily life, quietly influencing each step we take. When these habits are aligned with our personal goals, they become powerful tools that propel us forward rather than subtle anchors weighing us down.

At the heart of this alignment is self-awareness. It involves taking a deeper look inside, understanding what truly matters, and why those things matter. This introspective process begins with asking bold questions: What are my true goals? What drives my ambition and colors my perceptions? When you understand your personal aspirations with clarity, the habits needed to achieve them come into sharper focus. It's not just about setting habits— it's about creating habits that serve as stepstools to your aspirations.

Consider the habit of reading daily. For one individual, this could be essential for building knowledge in their career field, aligning perfectly with professional growth goals. For another, it could be a way to unwind and nurture creativity, reinforcing personal goals of achieved balance and emotional well-being. Here lies the beauty of personal growth: the same habit can have different meanings and alignments, reflecting the diverse tapestry of individual aspirations.

Aligning habits isn't only about fostering personal ambitions. It's also about pruning those routines that do not serve your purpose. Imagine nurturing new plant growth by removing weeds and debris. When you identify habits that stand in direct conflict with your goals, it becomes vital to reassess and redirect your energies. This might mean placing keen attention on breaking habits that sap your time and productivity, replacing them with those that feed into your overarching personal narrative.

The process of aligning habits with goals can empower personal resolve, igniting passion and motivation. Think about this synergy as a dynamic interplay between desire and action, where each positive habit actively feeds into your overall vision. This creates a powerful feedback loop. As small changes take root, they blossom into new opportunities, further reinforcing the connection between today's actions and tomorrow's achievements.

Initiating this alignment might feel overwhelming, but remember: it's important to start with small, manageable changes. This is akin to steering a large ship—a slight adjustment creates a new trajectory over time. Small efforts can lead to profound shifts. Begin by integrating two or three new habits directly related to your primary goal, tapping into the power of incremental change. This approach not only makes the process feel more manageable but can also build confidence and momentum.

Importantly, fostering a mindset oriented toward growth and learning enriches this journey. When habits align with personal goals, they continuously push boundaries, challenge assumptions, and inspire new pathways of thinking. Embrace the lessons learned from the process—both successes and setbacks. These experiences cultivate resilience and adaptability, reinforcing the resolve needed to stick with these habits during times of challenge.

Community and support systems play crucial roles too. Sharing goals and finding accountability partners who can support or challenge you creates an environment ripe for growth. Imagine engaging with a trusted mentor or peer group, individuals who celebrate your progress and reflect on setbacks with you. Their perspectives can be invaluable in keeping you centered and aligned with your personal aims.

Reflect regularly, adjusting and realigning as needed. Personal goals evolve; they shift with time and experience. As such, the habits that support these goals should be scrutinized and modified to stay relevant. Regular reflection acts as a compass. It provides insights into what's working and what isn't, ensuring that your journey remains true to your intended path. Use tools like journaling to assess progress, or establish periodic check-ins to reevaluate your stance and redefine your trajectory.

The journey of aligning habits with personal goals is not linear. It's a continual cycle of intention, action, reflection, and adaptation. Remember to celebrate small victories along the way. Recognizing the milestones that signify progress toward your goals reinforces your commitment and confidence in your ability to transform ambition into reality.

In conclusion, the deliberate alignment of habits with personal goals is a fundamental act of personal empowerment. It transforms habits from passive patterns into active agents of change. As these habits begin to resonate with your deepest desires, they create a powerful mechanism for personal growth. Let this alignment serve as a guiding star, illuminating the path toward achieving the fullness of your potential.

Chapter 8: The Role of Environment

Environment profoundly shapes our habits, often in ways we don't readily perceive. It's not just about the physical space but also the mental and emotional landscape we cultivate. When we consciously design our surroundings—organizing our workspace to reduce clutter or setting up reminders for our goals—we create conditions that can either propel us forward or hold us back. A supportive environment acts as a silent partner, constantly nudging us towards our aspirations and minimizing friction. For instance, simply placing your running shoes by the door can make the decision to exercise easier, transforming a small decision into a lasting habit. In essence, by altering our environment to align with our goals, we empower ourselves to make choices that support personal growth and productivity naturally and effortlessly. As we move forward, let's consider how cultivating an intentional environment can serve as a powerful catalyst for change, seamlessly integrating new routines into our lives.

Creating a Supportive Space

In the journey of personal development and transformation, the role of environment often shines as a pivotal yet sometimes overlooked element in shaping our habits. Our surroundings, whether physical, social, or digital, act as the backdrop against which our aspirations play out. Creating a supportive space isn't merely about making small tweaks; it's about crafting an environment that actively propels you toward the version of yourself you wish to become.

Imagine walking into a well-organized, inspiring workspace every day. It feels welcoming and motivates you to dive into your tasks with enthusiasm. This transformation doesn't happen by chance but by design. A supportive space invites productivity with open arms, and it's more than clean desks and tidy bookshelves. It's about cultivating an atmosphere where distractions are minimized and focus becomes effortless.

How do you begin crafting such an environment? Start by examining the physical spaces you occupy regularly. Are they cluttered or clear? Consider how your immediate surroundings align with your goals. Minimalism may be a trend, but reducing clutter is about creating mental clarity and physical efficiency, allowing your environment to work with you, not against you.

Think of your environment as an ally. It should be configured to encourage the habits you aspire to adopt and support the routines you've strategically planned. If your goal is to read more, position books in your line of sight. If healthier eating is a target, organize your pantry in a way that makes nutritious choices more accessible. It's the small, intentional changes that cumulatively create a space conducive to growth.

Interestingly, the paths to transformative environments needn't be grandiose. A shift as simple as altering furniture placement can shift the dynamics of a room. For instance, facing a desk towards a window might inspire bursts of creativity, while a well-placed lamp could boost focus during late-night work sessions. Every tweak should reflect a conscious decision aligning with your aspirations.

Beyond the immediate physical environment, our digital spaces, too, influence our habits. Consider the apps and tools you frequently engage with. Are they set up to aid your goals or derail them? Streamlining your digital life involves decluttering your devices of unnecessary distractions, organizing files systematically, and even setting up reminders that prompt you towards beneficial actions, enabling your digital ecosystem to mirror your intentions.

Creating a supportive space is also about managing the social aspects of your environment. Who you surround yourself with can either propel you to greatness or pull you back into old habits. Curate your social circle to include those who challenge you constructively, support your endeavors, and uplift your spirit. This doesn't mean severing ties, but rather fostering connections that contribute to a nourishing environment.

In this endeavor, it might help to establish designated zones for specific activities within your home or office. Build clear boundaries that signal to your brain the shift in activities, enhancing focus and efficiency. Whether it's a cozy nook for reading, a dedicated desk for work, or a serene space for meditation, these zones create a seamless transition between your various roles and responsibilities.

Moreover, don't forget to infuse your space with elements that resonate with your values and motivations. Whether it's artwork, music, or colors that inspire you, these personal touches make your environment not just supportive, but reflective of your unique identity. Here, consistency meets creativity, blending functionality with personal aesthetic.

Let's not underestimate the power of routine checks and adjustments. As you evolve, your environment should evolve with you. Periodically assess whether your space supports your current goals or if it requires reconfiguration. Adapting your environment while staying attuned to changes in your personal growth ensures its continuous alignment with your ambitions.

In sum, crafting a supportive space is an ongoing process, one that demands introspection and action in equal measure. It's about setting the stage for the life you envision, where your surroundings serve not as background noise but as a symphony harmonizing with your pursuit of greatness. As your journey unfolds, remember: every corner, every detail, sings the story of your intentional path toward mastery.

Minimizing External Distractions

In the journey of personal development and productivity, the environment plays a crucial role. Our surroundings can either support our goals or act as opposing forces that lead us astray. Minimizing external distractions is not merely about removing clutter or turning off notifications. It's about creating an intentional space that fosters focus and creativity, enabling us to harness our potential in meaningful ways.

Think about the last time you tried to concentrate on an important task but found yourself constantly interrupted. Whether it's the allure of social media, an overflowing inbox, or even the sound of traffic outside your window, distractions can break our flow, making it difficult to reengage with the task at hand. Recognizing these external distractors is the first step toward reclaiming control over our environment.

External distractions often masquerade as innocuous elements in our daily lives. A phone left unattended, a TV murmuring in the background, or even a cluttered desk can subtly, yet powerfully, impact our ability to maintain focus. These elements dilute our attention and energy, taking us away from important tasks and derailing our progress.

Creating a distraction-free zone requires a deliberate approach. To begin with, assess your current space and identify common culprits that disrupt your attention. Is your desk scattered with unrelated items? Do you have a habit of leaving the TV on for background noise? Are notifications constantly pinging on your devices? Each identified distraction is an opportunity to construct an environment that aligns with your productivity goals.

One effective strategy is to designate a specific area in your home or office solely for focused work. This doesn't have to be a separate room; even a dedicated corner can suffice. Keep this space sacred and free from unrelated activities. By doing so, you condition your mind to associate this area with concentration and productivity.

Beyond physical space, digital distractions pose a significant challenge in our modern lives. Our devices are designed to capture our attention, making it crucial to set boundaries. Implementing strategies like silencing unnecessary notifications, using website blockers during work hours, and scheduling specific times for checking emails or social media can drastically reduce digital interruptions.

It's also worthwhile to consider the auditory environment. Some people find absolute silence to be ideal for focus, while others thrive with ambient noise. If the latter is true for you, consider using apps or sound machines that generate consistent background sounds, which can mask disruptive noises and aid concentration.

Moreover, don't underestimate the power of visual simplicity. A cluttered space often mirrors a cluttered mind. Regularly tidying your workspace can free up mental resources, allowing you to think more clearly and creatively. Simplicity in your environment encourages a clean mental slate from which ideas can flow effortlessly.

However, it's important to approach the process of minimizing external distractions with warmth and self-compassion. Don't strive for a perfection that isn't sustainable. Recognize that some days will naturally present more challenges than others. The goal is not to eliminate every possible distraction but to manage them so that they no longer control you or steal your productivity.

Incorporating breaks into your routine is another valuable tactic. Our brains are not wired for prolonged concentration. Scheduling regular intervals to step away from intensive work can boost endurance and creativity. During these breaks, indulge in activities that refresh your mind and body—take a walk, meditate, or simply breathe deeply.

Lastly, enlist the support of those around you. Explain your need for undisturbed time to family, friends, or colleagues, and invite them to support your focus efforts. This might mean establishing quiet hours during the workday or sharing a mutual understanding that important tasks require undivided attention.

By actively shaping your environment, both physically and digitally, you create a space that reflects and nurtures your goals and aspirations. Remember, the pursuit of minimizing distractions isn't about deprivation but about reclaiming your power to focus on what truly matters. In this space, your potential becomes realized, and your capacity for growth and productivity expands.

Chapter 9: The Impact of Social Influences

Our social environment can be a powerful catalyst for change or a formidable barrier against it, playing a significant role in shaping our habits. When surrounded by individuals who uplift and support us, we're often inspired to reach new heights and break boundaries we thought were insurmountable. Peers who cheer on our every success and hold us accountable during slips provide a foundation for sustained growth. Yet, not all social influences are positive. Negative influences, like those imposing peer pressure or encouraging detrimental behaviors, can impede our progress. Recognizing these dynamics is key. By consciously choosing our social circles and actively engaging with communities that align with our personal goals, we can leverage the power of social influence to transform our habits and ultimately, our lives.

Leveraging Peer Support

When it comes to transforming our habits, we often overlook the profound impact of the social networks we inhabit. At the core of our society is an intricate web of relationships and interactions that subtly guide our behaviors and shape our goals. Whether it's a friend who encourages us to persevere or a group that shares similar ambitions, peer support can act as a powerful catalyst for personal change and growth.

Imagine embarking on a journey toward mastering a new habit. Alone, the path may seem steep, and the obstacles insurmountable. But with supportive peers, each step can become more manageable, each challenge less daunting. This isn't merely anecdotal; research consistently demonstrates that individuals are significantly more likely to adopt and maintain new behaviors when they are supported by others.

Consider the concept of accountability. Humans are inherently social creatures, wired to seek connection and approval. When we openly share our goals with peers, we create a sense of accountability that motivates us to uphold our commitments. In essence, it's not just about letting ourselves down—it's about letting down others who support our journey. This social accountability can be an extremely effective tool in overcoming inertia and moving toward personal development.

Peer support can come in many forms, from casual check-ins to formalized groups with structured meetings. An example of the latter is weight loss or sobriety support groups, which provide a platform for individuals to share successes, setbacks, and strategies. These groups create a communal environment that fosters encouragement and a sense of belonging, motivating members to adhere to their objectives.

However, the power of peer support isn't limited to organized groups. Even informal gatherings—such as a weekly run with friends or a shared challenge in the workplace—can create a positive ripple effect. When we engage with others who share our goals, the collective energy and enthusiasm can drive us forward. Shared experiences foster camaraderie and inspire persistence, even in adversity.

One of the most significant benefits of peer support is the opportunity for shared learning. Within a supportive community, individuals can exchange strategies and insights that might not have been apparent when tackling a habit alone. If someone has successfully navigated obstacles similar to your own, their wisdom can illuminate alternative paths to success. In this way, peer support becomes not just a network for emotional and motivational backing but a wellspring of practical knowledge that accelerates personal growth.

Practicing vulnerability within a peer support system is another crucial aspect that can strengthen our efforts to change. When we are open about our struggles, it invites empathy and shared humanity into our relationships. Acknowledging difficulties openly offers others the chance to provide constructive support and reinforce our perseverance. Brene Brown, a leading expert on vulnerability, highlights how engaging in truthful and open communication fosters connections—ties that can bolster our resolve to change and improve.

The leveraging of peer support is not without its potential pitfalls. Negative influences can sometimes masquerade as support or lead us down paths that deviate from our true objectives. Navigating peer dynamics requires discernment—being able to distinguish those who genuinely uplift from those whose presence may unwittingly hinder progress. It's vital to cultivate relationships that nurture your growth philosophy and align with your personal goals.

Start by identifying peers who reflect the values and aspirations you hold dear. Surrounding yourself with individuals committed to their own personal development can infuse your journey with positivity and drive. By consciously curating a supportive environment, you position yourself to benefit from healthy social dynamics while minimizing exposure to potential negativity.

Additionally, creating a reciprocal ecosystem of support can amplify the benefits of peer influence. When you encourage and assist others in their endeavors, it fortifies bonds and generates a culture of mutual growth. You contribute not only to their success but also to an atmosphere that promotes collective flourishing, which, in turn, propels your own ambitions.

Realizing the full potential of peer support extends beyond mere engagement with others. It necessitates active participation and intentionality. Be proactive in reaching out, initiating conversations, and inviting feedback. The more you invest in fostering authentic connections, the more robust the support system becomes.

Consider incorporating formal strategies to leverage peer support effectively. Forming mastermind groups or accountability pairs within focused areas of personal development provides structure and regularity. Scheduling regular check-ins keeps momentum alive and ensures that progress is consistently measured and celebrated.

In conclusion, leveraging peer support in the pursuit of transforming habits underscores a crucial truth: change is rarely a solitary endeavor. Our social connections are instrumental in shaping our journey, providing both the fuel and the compass to navigate the complexities of personal growth. By embedding ourselves in strong and positive networks, we harness a powerful force that propels us toward achieving more—and ultimately becoming the best versions of ourselves.

Navigating Negative Influences

In the complex tapestry of our lives, social influences play a pivotal role in shaping our behaviors and decisions. While supportive peers can propel us toward growth, negative influences can just as easily derail our progress. But what do we mean by "negative influences"? These are the subtle or overt pressures that lead us away from our personal goals and values, like a ship caught in an unseen current. Recognizing and navigating these forces is crucial for anyone aiming to build and sustain positive habits.

Negative influences can manifest in countless ways. They might come from coworkers who encourage procrastination, friends who downplay the importance of your wellness goals, or societal norms that make unhealthy behaviors seem acceptable. What's important is not just identifying these influences but understanding how they subtly erode your resolve. The whispers of "just once won't hurt" or "everyone else is doing it" are familiar refrains that beguile us into a false sense of security.

Overcoming the pull of negative influences begins with self-awareness. Without self-awareness, we might unconsciously mimic behaviors that conflict with our aspirations. Take the time to reflect on situations where you've veered off course. Was it the sway of groupthink, or perhaps the unsolicited advice from a well-meaning friend? Delve into these moments with an objective lens, acknowledging the external voices that drowned out your inner one.

Empathy is a powerful tool in this journey. It's easy to blame others for derailing our progress, but empathizing with their motivations can provide clarity. Maybe your friend suggesting another drink just wanted to prolong a fun evening or your colleague pushing back deadlines was stressed about their workload. Understanding doesn't excuse the behavior, but it helps you create strategies to counteract such influences without alienating people.

Once you've identified the negative influences, setting boundaries is your next step. Boundaries are not about building walls but creating a protective space where your goals can thrive. Communicate your commitments clearly, whether it's declining an indulgent meal that conflicts with your health goals or politely refusing to engage in gossip that drags you emotionally. A firm, yet considerate approach helps others respect your path and keeps you on track without resentment building on either side.

You'll also find power in aligning yourself with like-minded individuals. Just as negative influences can hinder growth, positive peers can amplify it. Seek out communities that elevate your aspirations, whether it's a fitness group, professional network, or book club. These allies will provide both encouragement and accountability. When you surround yourself with people striving for similar goals, you create an environment that naturally repels negative influences.

Don't underestimate the impact of your personal environment as well. The spaces we occupy daily aren't neutral; they shape our mental and emotional states. Craft a space at home and work that mirrors your ambitions. This could mean organizing your workspace to minimize distractions or setting up a home gym area to encourage regular workouts. When your environment aligns with your intentions, it acts as a silent partner in resisting negative influences.

However, sometimes the most insidious influences come from within. Our inner critic can echo societal pressures, casting doubt on our capabilities and feeding self-sabotage. To navigate these internal influences, embrace practices that reinforce self-compassion and resilience. Journaling, meditation, or affirmations can help you reframe negative self-talk and strengthen your commitment to personal growth.

Learning to navigate negative influences is not a one-time effort but an ongoing journey. It requires vigilance, reflection, and adjustments as new situations and people enter your life. Commit to regular self-check-ins, assessing how well you're managing the influences around you and within you. These moments of introspection can reveal surprising insights and areas for improvement. Over time, you'll notice a shift, where resilience becomes instinctual, and the lure of detrimental influences fades.

The strength you gain from navigating negative influences isn't just personal. It empowers you to become a positive influence in the lives of others. As you build habits rooted in authenticity and resilience, you model possibilities for friends, family, and colleagues navigating similar challenges. Your journey becomes a beacon, inviting others to break free from the grip of negativity and envision a path dictated by choice rather than chance.

In closing, remember this: It's not about eliminating negative influences entirely—that's an impossible task—but about skillfully navigating them. By doing so, you reclaim the power to steer your life toward your true desires. Each thoughtful boundary, aligned relationship, and mindful decision creates a ripple effect, advancing you steadily toward a life crafted intentionally, passionately, and freely.

Chapter 10: Tracking Progress and Making Adjustments

Embarking on a journey of personal transformation is as much about the journey as it is about the destination. As you work to change your habits, tracking your progress becomes essential. This process isn't just about measuring success; it's about fostering awareness of your own growth. By keenly observing patterns and embracing flexibility, you empower yourself to refine your routines and make necessary adjustments. This journey of self-discovery demands conscious effort and the willingness to adapt, highlighting areas where improvements can evolve incrementally. The key is to balance patience with persistence, understanding that progress isn't always linear. Use various tools and techniques to monitor your habits effectively; this paves the way for meaningful adjustments that better align with your evolving goals. Through intentional tracking, you'll uncover insights that guide adaptable, resilient habit formation, propelling you closer to a more fulfilling and productive life.

Tools for Monitoring Habits

As we embark on the journey of habit transformation, it's crucial to have the right tools at our disposal. These tools not only help us track our progress but also illuminate patterns that may have gone unnoticed. Monitoring habits isn't just about keeping tabs on our actions; it's about understanding our behaviors, tweaking our strategies, and ultimately, steering ourselves towards personal growth.

An effective way to begin is with activity tracking applications. These digital tools are designed specifically to assist in monitoring daily routines and provide insights into our behavioral patterns. They offer features like goal setting, reminders, and progress graphs. While some people may find their sleek interfaces engaging, others might prefer a more tactile approach. This is where traditional methods, like journaling, come into play. The process of writing by hand can be surprisingly clarifying—it forces us to slow down and reflect on our day's actions. It turns the abstract into concrete evidence of our successes and areas that need focus.

For those inclined towards technology, habit-tracking apps offer a convenient and efficient way to document habits. Many of these apps are equipped with analytics features that provide statistics and trends. This quantitative feedback is invaluable, as it allows us to see how consistent we truly are over time. With this data, we can identify which habits are sticking and which ones are not, enabling us to make informed adjustments.

But not all tools need to be digital. Analog tools, like a simple calendar system, can serve as a powerful visual reminder and motivator. Marking a big "X" on each day your new habit is completed can become a satisfying ritual. This method, often referred to as the "Seinfeld Strategy," underscores the power of visual streaks and can be hugely encouraging. Seeing a chain of successful days builds momentum, which can be a potent driver in ensuring consistency.

In addition to these individualized methods, peer accountability plays a crucial role. Sharing your habit journey with a friend or a group can introduce a layer of commitment that goes beyond self-monitoring. Knowing that someone else is aware of your goals adds a degree of responsibility, and the encouragement or constructive criticism from peers can be incredibly motivating.

When selecting tools, it's vital to choose those that resonate with personal preferences and lifestyle. If your workspace is cluttered with notifications, a tangible planner might offer the respite needed to focus on yourself. Alternatively, if your mobile device is your go-to for organization, a high-functioning app could seamlessly integrate habit tracking into your daily routine.

Having discussed various tools, one fundamental step remains—regular review. Carving out time to periodically review your tools and methods is as important as the tools themselves. During these reviews, it's valuable to ask reflective questions: Are the current tools still effective? Do they motivate me? Am I seeing the changes I set out to achieve? These introspections help in fine-tuning the system and maintaining momentum.

In the end, the tools for monitoring habits are more than just mechanisms for measure—they are allies in our quest for improvement. By leveraging these instruments wisely, you create a framework that not only tracks your journey but also inspires confidence and fosters resilience. Through diligent monitoring and insightful adjustments, the journey to mastering habits becomes not just a possibility but a thriving reality.

Adjusting Routines for Better Results

Our lives are a conglomeration of routines, often leading us down predestined paths. However, the beauty of routines lies in their malleability. When you track your progress, the insights gained act as a compass, guiding you to make necessary adjustments. The ability to tweak these routines is a powerful skill. It allows you to align your daily actions with your ambitions, ensuring that you're perpetually on course towards personal growth and development.

Adjusting routines doesn't mean a complete overhaul. Small, deliberate changes can yield substantial results. Consider the notion of incorporating micro-adjustments. By making incremental improvements, you can maintain the momentum necessary for sustained transformation. For example, if you're working on enhancing your productivity, identifying nonessential tasks that consume valuable time is critical. Allocate that time instead to activities that contribute directly to your goals.

The process of routine adjustment is deeply personal. What works for one person might not for another. It's essential to maintain a spirit of experimentation. Try different approaches and note how they impact your routines. This sense of curiosity and openness can often lead to unexpected breakthroughs and more efficient ways of approaching everyday tasks.

Remember, not every change will stick immediately. Some will require fine-tuning, patience, and perseverance. It's important to recognize that setbacks are not failures but opportunities to learn and refine your approach. By developing an adaptive mindset, you become resilient, capable of gracefully navigating the ebbs and flows that accompany any journey of personal growth.

Feedback is another invaluable tool in adjusting routines. It can come from self-reflection or from trusted friends and mentors who understand your goals. By analyzing this feedback thoughtfully, you can identify patterns that may need adjusting. This also fosters a sense of accountability, encouraging you to stay aligned with your objectives.

The impact of even minor adjustments can be transformative. You might find new energy and motivation, invigorating those mundane aspects of daily life that often feel burdensome. As routines become more aligned with your aspirations, they generate a positive feedback loop, where small successes breed further enthusiasm and commitment.

Moreover, an effective adjustment often involves being proactive about potential obstacles. Identifying possible pitfalls before they arise gives you the opportunity to devise strategies for overcoming them. If you know that you're likely to hit a mid-afternoon slump, perhaps a brisk walk or a short meditation session could counteract this dip in energy and focus.

It's crucial to periodically review and adjust your routines based on current priorities and life changes. What served you well a year ago might not fit your present circumstances. Life is dynamic, and so too should be our routines. Embrace change as a catalyst for ensuring your habits remain relevant and reflective of your true self.

Ultimately, the goal of adjusting routines isn't just about better results today. It's about crafting a life that's resilient to change and aligned with your greatest potential. With each small adjustment, you're not only enhancing your present but also paving a richer, more fulfilling path into the future.

Chapter 11: Real-Life Stories of Habit Transformation

In the heart of habit transformation lies the power of personal journeys, filled with determination and growth. Consider the story of Sarah, who felt trapped in a cycle of procrastination and self-doubt, unable to move forward in her career. Once she recognized her unproductive habits, Sarah committed to a modest yet life-changing routine—waking up thirty minutes earlier every day to plan her tasks. Over time, this small shift rewired her mindset, instilling confidence and discipline. Meanwhile, John, a middle-aged father, sought to overcome his sedentary lifestyle for better health. Inspired by his children, he started with a simple pledge to walk ten minutes daily, which gradually evolved into marathon training. These real-life stories of transformation remind us that the journey to change often begins with small, mindful steps and grows into extraordinary achievements, showcasing that no habit is too ingrained to alter. As these narratives unfold, they reveal valuable insights into perseverance and the incredible potential for change within us all.

Inspiring Personal Narratives

In the journey of habit transformation, real-life stories resonate with a power that's often unmatched by mere theory. They illuminate the infinite possibilities that arise when determination meets the right strategies. These narratives of ordinary individuals achieving extraordinary change illustrate not just what is possible, but how it's done. From small town schools to bustling city offices, these stories serve as beacons of motivation, reminding us that anyone can shape a new destiny by transforming their habits.

Consider Jane, a working mom who felt overwhelmed by the demands of her career and home life. Every day, she struggled to balance her professional duties with the unyielding needs of her young children. Jane's story begins with her feeling trapped, her energy constantly drained by a never-ending cycle of tasks. A chance encounter at a seminar on habit-building prompted her to rethink her approach to daily routines. She started by waking up just thirty minutes earlier each day—a small change that allowed her to organize her thoughts and prepare for the day ahead. This simple shift led to improved time management, increased productivity, and ultimately, a more harmonious balance between work and family life.

Then there's Mark, an artist who'd lost his creative flame, buried under the weight of self-doubt and inconsistent habits. For years, unfinished canvases collected dust in his cramped studio. After hitting a personal and professional low, Mark decided something had to change. He began implementing a regimented routine, dedicating specific hours each day to his art, regardless of inspiration. This turned into a practice of discipline that summoned creativity even on the driest of days. Over time, this structured habit reshaped his mindset, reigniting a passion that expanded beyond the walls of his studio, influencing every aspect of his life.

In the bustling heart of New York City, Michael, a young entrepreneur, faced a common adversary: burnout. The relentless pursuit of success left him depleted, wondering if his entrepreneurial dream was worth the cost to his health. Motivated by a friend's success in transforming their life through habit changes, he decided to invest time in understanding his patterns. Michael discovered the importance of work-life balance and introduced mindful breaks throughout his day. His story is a testament that sometimes the boldest innovation is daring to pause and recalibrate. His renewed approach led to a healthier lifestyle and a more creative business approach, proving that nurturing personal well-being is vital for sustainable success.

On the other side of the globe, Priya, an academic researcher in India, found herself engulfed in a routine devoid of personal satisfaction. Her habits centered solely on work, leaving little time for self-care or leisure. The turning point came during a reflective walk on a family vacation, where the clear skies sparked an epiphany. Priya decided to incorporate small, meaningful changes into her daily life, such as short meditation sessions and nightly reading. This mindful approach enriched her mental landscape, enhancing not only her research productivity but also her quality of life.

Let's turn to Carlos, whose story revolves around overcoming physical limitations. Initially restricted by a severe back injury, Carlos struggled to maintain even the simplest physical activities. His remedy lay in cultivating a new habit: daily stretching and gentle exercises. While progress was slow, persistence was key. Carlos's journey exemplifies the power of patience and perspective; each day, he focused not on immediate results, but on long-term healing. As his strength returned, so did his confidence, and what began as a necessity evolved into a passionate hobby in fitness.

In these stories, the common thread is transformation born from the seeds of consistency and commitment. Each narrative is a real-world demonstration of how shifts in daily routines can lead to profound personal growth. They illustrate that within our habitual actions lies the inherent ability to redefine our life's direction.

These inspiring personal narratives echo the universal truth that change often begins with smaller steps. As individuals like Jane, Mark, Michael, Priya, and Carlos show, the most significant shifts often start with humble beginnings—a few minutes dedicated to a new practice, the courage to disrupt harmful routines, or the drive to redefine a life path. These changes underscore the notion that transformative habits are not about grand gestures but about sustained effort and dedication over time.

Exploring the victories and challenges of these individuals helps us grasp the essence of perseverance. The stories offer a glimpse into the resilience required to overcome setbacks and the joy of achieving personal milestones. They are reminders that failure is not a stopping point but a stepping stone on the journey of habit transformation.

As we soak in these accounts, it becomes clear that there is no singular path to habit metamorphosis. Each story is as unique as the individual narrating it, yet holds a universal lesson: consistent, intentional actions shape our reality. They remind us that while the path to change may be fraught with challenges and setbacks, it is also lined with the promise of rewards and greater self-awareness.

For those who seek change, these narratives provide both inspiration and blueprint. They serve as testaments to the power of persistence, prompting us to examine our own habits with renewed curiosity and resolve. Through their experiences, we are encouraged to embark on our own transformative journeys, equipped with the knowledge that profound change is always within reach, waiting to be unlocked by the habits we choose to cultivate each day.

Lessons Learned from Success and Failure

As we delve into the transformative power of habits, real-life stories provide valuable insights into the successes and failures of those who have traveled similar paths. Each story offers a piece of wisdom, a lesson learned that can guide others towards their own breakthroughs. What turns a simple intention into a lasting habit is a blend of perseverance, mindset, and adaptation. The journey is often a patchwork of triumphs and defeats, each teaching us something vital about our behavior.

Success in transforming habits often stems from an understanding that change is a gradual process. Many stories highlight how individuals initially attempted to overhaul their lives all at once, only to face overwhelming challenges. Through experience, they've learned that significant change is built on small, incremental steps. For example, rather than pledging to exercise every day, one might start with a manageable commitment, like a short daily walk. This approach not only makes the goal feel less daunting but also builds confidence with each small success.

Failure, while often viewed negatively, is an equally important teacher in habit transformation. It sheds light on the underlying issues that may have gone unnoticed otherwise. The process of failing and subsequently adjusting teaches resilience. When setbacks occur, they bring an opportunity to reassess and refine one's strategy, whether it means setting more realistic goals or identifying unnoticed triggers that derail progress.

Another lesson learned is the importance of self-compassion. Real-life stories reveal that those who bounce back from failure often exhibit a kind and forgiving attitude toward themselves. This doesn't mean excusing mistakes, but rather acknowledging them as part of the journey. By eschewing harsh self-criticism, they continue pursuing their goals without the paralyzing weight of guilt or disappointment.

The stories also emphasize the power of accountability. Individuals who succeed in transforming their habits frequently enlist the support of others. This support can come from friends, family, or even digital communities. Peer support can offer encouragement, share useful experiences, and provide a form of constructive pressure that helps maintain commitment to new habits. It's a lesson in the value of social structures to reinforce personal endeavors.

In contrast, many failures in habit change arise from underestimating the role of environment. Stories reveal that some individuals struggled to maintain new habits because their environments were filled with cues and temptations that triggered old behaviors. Successful habit changers learn to design their environments in ways that support their goals, removing obstacles and placing reminders or incentives that reinforce positive actions.

Moreover, the stories teach us about flexibility. Rigidity in routine can be a downfall, as life is inherently unpredictable. Those who succeed learn to adapt their habits in response to changing circumstances. For instance, a change in work schedule isn't seen as an insurmountable barrier but as a challenge to creatively adjust their routine. This adaptability ensures that progress can continue despite disruptions.

Some narratives emphasize the critical role of intrinsic motivation, demonstrating that sustainable habit change happens when the motivation is deeply personal. Individuals who align their habits with their core values and long-term aspirations find that staying on track becomes less of a chore and more of a fulfilling pursuit. This intrinsic motivation is often what rejuvenates commitment when external incentives or initial enthusiasm wane.

Listening to these stories reveals another subtle yet profound takeaway: the importance of celebrating small victories. Acknowledging progress, no matter how minor, reinforces a positive feedback loop. Celebrations act as milestones that provide encouragement and renew commitment, making the journey toward larger goals feel more achievable.

The intersection of habit transformation stories also highlights a profound recognition of time. Many individuals come to understand that lasting change doesn't adhere to a strict timeline. Patience becomes a crucial companion in the journey, where the focus shifts from immediate results to gradual improvement. This patience allows for steady growth and reduces the pressure that often leads to burnout or failure.

Finally, these narratives remind us that everyone's path is unique. Comparing oneself to others can be demotivating because it fails to account for personal circumstances and differences in challenges. Instead, these stories inspire a focus on individual progress, encouraging a personalized approach to habit transformation. Defining success based on personal benchmarks, rather than external standards, allows for a more authentic and meaningful journey.

In conclusion, real-life stories of habit transformation reveal a rich tapestry of lessons about the intricate dance of success and failure. They teach us about perseverance, the importance of environment, the power of peer support, and the need for flexibility and self-compassion. Embracing these lessons equips us not only to transform habits but to embark on a journey of personal growth with resilience and hope. By learning from those who have bravely shared their stories, we can craft our own narratives of change, fueled by the wisdom and insights gleaned from their experiences.

Chapter 12: Overcoming Setbacks

Setbacks are an inevitable part of any journey towards personal growth, but they don't define our path—instead, how we respond to them does. When relapses occur, it's crucial to recognize them not as failures but as opportunities for insight and learning. A temporary lapse in routine doesn't erase your progress; it enriches the path with valuable lessons. By embracing a mindset that seeks understanding from these moments, we can refine our strategies for rebound and recovery. Adjusting our sails, we harness the power of resilience to push forward stronger and wiser. Resilience isn't about unwavering perfection but the ability to adapt and continue despite challenges. Remember, achieving lasting change is a dynamic process, requiring compassion for yourself and the courage to continue the journey with renewed determination.

Managing Relapses

Embarking on the journey of habit change is both exciting and daunting, marked by victories and setbacks alike. It's important to remember that relapses aren't failures but rather a natural part of the process. They offer invaluable lessons and opportunities for growth, allowing you to delve deeper into the triggers and underlying reasons behind the change you seek. Understanding this can transform what initially feels like a step back into a powerful leap forward in your personal development journey.

One crucial aspect of managing relapses is acknowledging their inevitability. Even the most motivated individuals encounter moments where old patterns resurface. Instead of viewing these as signs of personal weakness, view them as experience to pinpoint precisely where your strategies might need refinement. This mindset shift can reframe your approach, turning self-criticism into self-compassion. By doing so, you create a foundation of resilience that better supports long-term change.

To effectively manage relapses, start by identifying the cues and triggers that lead to them. Often, external factors such as stress, environment, or social settings play significant roles. It can be helpful to maintain a journal, noting when relapses occur, and considering what may have preceded them. Analyzing this information lets you adjust your environment or strategies to minimize these triggers. This introspection isn't about avoiding responsibility but rather understanding your context to make informed adjustments.

Another technique is to structure your environment in a way that supports your goals, mitigating the temptation to revert to old habits. For instance, if you're working to reduce screen time, consider setting designated tech-free zones or times, allowing yourself space to explore alternative activities that align with your new habits. This proactive approach can create a physical and mental landscape that naturally favors your desired behaviors.

Moreover, fostering a support network can be crucial in managing relapses. Sharing your goals with friends, family, or a support group creates a sense of accountability and provides a source of encouragement when challenges arise. It's important to choose individuals who understand your journey and can offer genuine support rather than judgment. These relationships can be a lifeline, reinforcing your commitment to change when faced with the alluring pull of old habits.

Incorporating small, incremental changes rather than drastic ones can also reduce the frequency and impact of relapses. By building new habits gradually, you allow your brain more time to adjust, which can strengthen the changes over time. This approach respects the complexity of habit formation, giving your mind the time it needs to solidify new routines before additional changes are introduced.

Reflecting on past successes can also help manage relapses. When you find yourself facing a setback, remind yourself of the progress you've made. Reflecting on your accomplishments shifts focus away from the current relapse and instead highlights your ability to change.

Celebrate these small successes, using them as motivation to realign your efforts and continue forward.

Developing a plan for dealing with relapses is another vital strategy. By preemptively considering how you'll respond when a setback occurs, you equip yourself with a toolkit of strategies to counteract the relapse. This might include setting specific rules about returning to your new habit immediately, employing positive self-talk, or reaching out to your support network for encouragement.

Lastly, embracing a mindset of continuous growth and learning is crucial. Recognize that setbacks are not the end but rather a part of the journey. By maintaining a perspective that views setbacks as instructional, you promote a culture of learning within yourself. This perspective fosters resilience and adaptability, allowing you to grow stronger and more committed with each challenge you face.

Managing relapses is about understanding that change is a journey with many stages. Every step, including the missteps, contributes to a greater understanding of yourself and your patterns. By adopting strategies that focus on self-awareness and support, you transform setbacks into stepping stones, paving the way for lasting personal growth and habit mastery.

Strategies for Rebound and Recovery

Setbacks can often feel like an immovable wall suddenly placed on your path, blocking further progress. However, much like a skilled climber finds grip even on the steepest cliffs, we all possess the innate ability to overcome these barriers by bouncing back stronger than before. The journey of rebounding after a setback isn't just about regaining lost ground; it's an opportunity to gain new perspectives, reinforce resilience, and recalibrate towards goals with renewed vigor.

The first step in effective recovery is understanding that setbacks are not indicative of failure. They're merely a part of the learning curve. When we acknowledge setbacks as potential stepping stones rather than stumbling blocks, we begin to shift our perspective. This shift is critical; it transforms temporary brakes into strategic pauses that allow us to reassess, reflect, and revise our approach.

To foster a mindset primed for rebound, embrace self-compassion. Treat yourself with the same kindness you would offer a friend. Instead of dwelling on what went wrong, concentrate on what can be learned from the experience. This empathetic approach helps diminish self-criticism, fostering an environment where growth can occur. It's essential to give yourself permission to pause, process the emotions involved, and gather the courage to start anew.

The Power of Reflection

Reflection is an indispensable tool in the rebound toolkit. By carefully examining the events leading to the setback, you can identify patterns that contributed to it. Was it a lack of preparation, external influences, or perhaps an internal conflict bubbling beneath the surface? Once these are pinpointed, you can address them directly, ensuring they don't hinder your progress in the future.

Consider adopting a reflection journal if you haven't already. Documenting your thoughts not only aids in understanding emotional responses but also highlights specific actions that can be adjusted. Over time, this practice provides a resource-rich archive from which you can continually derive insights and strategies.

Taking Action

Once insights are gathered, action is essential. It's not enough to know why something went wrong; you need a plan to rectify it. Start by setting clear, attainable goals. Break down requisite actions into manageable steps, using past lessons to inform your new approach. This method not only makes the task less daunting but also provides a roadmap to track progress, which can be incredibly motivating.

As you layout your new plan, remember to build flexibility into your strategies. Life is unpredictable, and rigid plans can easily crumble under unexpected pressures. Creating room for adjustments allows you to navigate future setbacks with agility.

The Role of Support Systems

You don't have to face setbacks alone. One of the strongest assets in rebounding is having a solid support system. Whether it's confiding in a trusted friend or seeking guidance from a mentor, external perspectives can offer fresh insights and moral support. Sometimes, just knowing that someone believes in your ability to overcome can reignite your inner resolve.

Online communities and support groups can also serve as valuable resources. In these spaces, you're likely to encounter individuals who have weathered similar storms. Their experiences can offer both practical advice and emotional solidarity, reminding you that you're not alone in this journey.

Building Resilience Through Routine

Establishing a routine plays a pivotal role in recovery. Routine provides stability and predictability in times of chaos. Cultivating daily habits that align with your goals ensures that progress is continuous, even when setbacks disrupt. Whether it's dedicating fifteen minutes to mindful meditation each morning or a daily review of your progress list, these structured practices can ground you and keep the momentum going.

As you rebuild your routine, incorporate flexibility to allow for experimentation and recovery. Experiment with different approaches to see what resonates and supports your rebound best. Celebrating small victories along the way reinforces positive behavior, building a progressively more resilient mindset.

Maintaining a Growth Mindset

Central to a successful recovery is maintaining a growth mindset - the belief that capabilities can improve with time and effort. This mindset fuels perseverance through setbacks. By embracing challenges as opportunities to grow rather than obstacles to avoid, you're nurturing your ability to adapt and thrive in the face of adversity.

Challenge yourself to view each setback as a chance to build tolerance for discomfort and foster a thirst for discovering new solutions. Reframe obstacles as curious puzzles to be solved instead of insurmountable barriers.

Mindfulness and Emotional Regulation

Mindfulness, the practice of staying present, becomes invaluable during recovery. It sharpens your focus, helping you remain attuned to your actions and emotions. Mindfulness practices reduce stress, making it easier to approach solutions creatively and conciliatorily. Techniques such as mindful breathing or progressive relaxation help regulate emotional responses, preventing overwhelm and fostering clear-headed decision-making.

Consider integrating mindfulness into your daily life as a foundational strategy for long-term resilience. Whether it's through meditation, yoga, or mindful journaling, these practices help cultivate a steadiness of mind, enabling you to view setbacks with detachment rather than emotional reactivity.

Finally, remember that rebounding is a journey, not a destination. Each forward step, no matter how small, contributes to a larger outline of growth and transformation. Be patient and celebrate your progress. Recovery is not merely about regaining lost ground but evolving into a version of yourself better equipped to overcome future challenges. So take heart - with each setback, you're not starting from scratch; you're starting from experience, informed, and ready to tackle what's ahead.

Chapter 13: Habit Mastery in the Workplace

Building habits in the workplace isn't just about enhancing efficiency; it's about nurturing an environment where growth and collaboration thrive. We've all experienced the whirlwind of office demands and the pressure to perform at peak levels. By mastering productive habits, professionals can navigate this chaos with clarity and purpose. Such mastery involves consciously designing routines that align with both personal and organizational goals, ensuring that each task contributes to a broader vision of success. Consider how small changes, like structuring your day to tackle complex tasks when you're most alert, can compound over time to create formidable professional momentum. It's also about fostering a culture where employees feel empowered to share their strategies for success, creating a ripple effect of collective improvement. Habit mastery in the workplace is a transformative journey where individual efforts fuel a shared mission, and every action becomes a step toward not just personal achievement, but organizational excellence.

Enhancing Professional Efficiency

In the ever-evolving landscape of the workplace, professional efficiency stands as a cornerstone of success. Amidst deadlines, meetings, and the constant influx of information, finding ways to enhance your efficiency isn't just advantageous—it's essential. For many, the key lies in habit mastery, a focused and intentional approach to shaping the way we work. By adjusting our habits, we can transform daily routines into powerful catalysts for productivity and personal growth.

Efficiency in the workplace hinges on understanding the difference between being busy and being productive. It's easy to fill your day with tasks and leave the office feeling exhausted without achieving significant outcomes. By identifying and cultivating the right habits, you create a framework that prioritizes impactful work over mere activity. The goal is to streamline processes, reduce time spent on low-value tasks, and increase capacity for strategic thinking and innovation.

Start by examining your current work habits. What patterns do you notice? Do you tend to procrastinate on challenging assignments until the last minute, or perhaps you spend too much time perfecting low-priority tasks? Recognizing these tendencies is the first step towards creating change. The objective is to replace non-constructive habits with routines that drive efficiency, like tackling high-impact tasks first or dedicating specific times for deep, focused work.

Another powerful habit that enhances professional efficiency is setting clear, achievable goals. When you define what success looks like for each project or task, you provide yourself with a roadmap that guides daily actions. Goals should be specific and time-bound, allowing you to track progress and make necessary adjustments. This approach fosters a sense of accomplishment and momentum, encouraging continued effort and focus.

Time management strategies are fundamental to boosting efficiency. Techniques such as the Pomodoro Technique, where work is divided into short, focused intervals followed by a break, can significantly enhance concentration and productivity. Adopting habits that encourage regular reviews of your priorities can also be transformative. By periodically assessing what truly matters, you can ensure your efforts are aligned with both personal and organizational objectives.

Communication plays a pivotal role in workplace efficiency. Developing habits that facilitate clear and concise communication can prevent misunderstanding and streamline collaboration. Whether it's setting a daily agenda, providing quick updates, or establishing a feedback loop, effective communication habits can lead to smoother operations and faster decision-making.

Moreover, building a habit of reflection can be immensely beneficial. Taking time at the end of each day to contemplate what went well, what could be improved, and how you can adjust your approach moving forward helps create a cycle of continuous learning and improvement. This practice not only cultivates self-awareness but also equips you with the insights needed to enhance overall efficiency.

Incorporating technology wisely into your work habits can also drive efficiency. Tools that automate repetitive tasks or facilitate data organization can free up valuable time, allowing you to focus on more strategic initiatives. The key is to adopt technology purposefully, ensuring it complements your workflow rather than complicates it.

Your work environment significantly impacts your habits and efficiency. Creating a space that reduces distractions, whether digital or physical, fosters concentration and creativity. Simple changes like organizing your workspace, setting boundaries for interruptions, or even arranging your work schedule to align with your natural energy levels can make a remarkable difference in your productivity.

Additionally, learning to say no is an underrated but powerful habit. By carefully selecting where to spend your time and energy, you preserve your resources for tasks that truly matter. This skill involves assessing requests objectively and making decisions that align with your overarching goals, ensuring your efficiency isn't compromised by overcommitment.

The journey towards enhanced professional efficiency isn't without challenges. Resistance to change is natural, and it's essential to approach habit transformation with patience and persistence. Small, incremental changes often yield the most sustainable results. Celebrate your successes, no matter how minor, to maintain motivation and build momentum.

Finally, remember that enhancing professional efficiency is not about working harder, but working smarter. It's about aligning your habits with your goals and values to create a work life that is not only efficient but also fulfilling. As you continue to master your habits, you'll find that the benefits extend beyond productivity, enhancing both your professional journey and your personal development.

Fostering a Productive Work Environment

In the bustling corridors of modern workplaces, the dynamics of productivity are heavily influenced by the environment we cultivate. A productive work environment isn't just about organized desks and the hum of efficient machinery; it's an ecosystem where habits thrive, communication flourishes, and innovation is encouraged. The key to habit mastery in the workplace rests in how well we can engineer this environment to amplify our professional potential.

Establishing a productive work environment starts with understanding the integral role that physical space plays in shaping our habits. An office set up to optimize worker comfort and minimize unnecessary distractions can significantly boost collective productivity. Picture a workspace where light streams naturally through wide windows, the background is a calming hue, and the air smells fresh, not sterile. Each of these elements subtly influences our mood and focus, pushing us gently toward a more mindful and deliberate work ethic.

The physical setup, however, is only a part of the equation. The organizational culture that permeates these walls profoundly impacts how habits are nurtured and sustained. Organizations that prioritize openness and innovation enable employees to experiment with their routines, find what works best for them, and adapt accordingly. Think of an environment where bosses are approachable, discussions are encouraged, and every failure is treated as a step toward success. Such an atmosphere doesn't just foster productivity; it breeds loyalty, creativity, and resilience.

A crucial aspect of fostering a productive environment is the notion of psychological safety. Employees need to feel secure in their roles, willing to take calculated risks without the fear of reprimand. In this kind of atmosphere, individuals are more likely to share ideas, provide feedback, and engage fully with their tasks. This openness leads to the development of more efficient habits, as team members feel comfortable challenging the status quo and suggesting improvements.

Furthermore, the role of leadership can't be understated in developing a productive work environment. Leaders set the tone and standard for workplace behavior and habits. They can model the productive habits they wish to see in their teams by exemplifying efficiency, respect, and dedication. When leaders practice good habits, such as punctuality, transparency, and responsiveness, they're not just reinforcing productivity; they're inspiring it.

Consider also the importance of technology in shaping the modern work environment. Leveraging the right tools can automate mundane tasks, allowing employees to focus on higher-value work that requires creativity and strategy. Programs that streamline communication, project management, and data analysis let teams concentrate on what truly matters. It's about constructing a digital landscape that supports rather than stifles productivity.

However, to truly nurture a productive work environment, there must be room for flexibility. Rigidity can stifle creativity and innovation. Allowing employees the liberty to adjust their work habits according to their personal lives' demands can yield surprising boosts in output. Flexible hours, remote work options, and customizable office spaces are just a few ways organizations can cater to diverse work styles and needs.

Collaboration is another cornerstone of a productive work environment. Encouraging teamwork can diminish the silos that often hinder company-wide efficiency. When employees work together, blending ideas and skills, they're more likely to innovate and escalate the organization's productivity. Regular team meetings, cross-departmental projects, and communal spaces can foster such a culture of cooperation.

Mindfulness and well-being also play significant roles. Stress, burnout, and fatigue are productivity killers. Creating spaces for relaxation, promoting work-life balance, and encouraging regular breaks ensure that employees can recharge and return to work with renewed energy and focus. Consider integrating small wellness initiatives—like meditation sessions or fitness classes—into daily routines to promote a culture that values both mental and physical health.

Finally, it's imperative to keep the lines of communication open. Feedback loops, where employees can freely express their thoughts about the work environment and their personal habits, are essential. This continuous cycle of input and change keeps the environment dynamic and adaptable. Use regular surveys, suggestion boxes, and one-on-one meetings to gather insights and make necessary adjustments.

In essence, fostering a productive work environment involves a holistic approach that ties physical, cultural, and technological elements together. It requires intentional actions to build a space where employees not only perform their duties efficiently but also feel motivated and supported. By focusing on these areas, organizations can transform their environments into powerful incubators for habit mastery and peak productivity. Optimizing the workplace is not merely about pushing for output metrics; it is about creating a nurturing space for each employee to flourish and contribute sustainably.

Chapter 14: Long-Term Maintenance and Adaptation

In the lifelong journey of transforming our habits, a critical aspect is not just establishing them but maintaining and adapting them as life evolves. Achieving this requires more than simple repetition; it demands a resilient mindset and a readiness to pivot when necessary. As we experience changes in our environments, responsibilities, and even our own aspirations, the habits we adopt must be just as dynamic, evolving in sync with our growth. It's about embracing an adventurous approach, open to exploring different paths while staying committed to our core objectives. Sustaining beneficial habits means continually reinforcing the patterns that serve us, while also having the courage to let go of those that don't fit our current context. This balance ensures that our habits remain a supportive scaffold, empowering us to thrive amidst the inevitable shifts and turns of life.

Sustaining Beneficial Habits Over Time

Sustaining beneficial habits over time is kind of like nurturing a plant. At first, you water it diligently and give it all the sunlight it needs. But gradually, it becomes a part of your environment, just requiring occasional attention to keep thriving. The same goes for the habits we've painstakingly built. They begin as conscious decisions but with consistency, they blend into our daily lives seamlessly. It's important, however, not to become complacent. Maintenance is key; even the most deeply rooted habits need a bit of care now and then to stay vibrant and effective.

The essence of sustaining a habit long-term lies in understanding the ebb and flow of motivation. Motivation is our initial drive, the spark that gets us started. Still, it naturally fluctuates. Some days, enthusiasm fuels our actions, while other days might feel like wading through mud. Here is where discipline becomes crucial. Discipline is what remains when excitement wanes. Instead of relying solely on motivation, intertwine discipline with structured routines and environments that support your goals. Over time, you'll find that persistence is more about gentle adaptability than unwavering effort.

Let's delve into the importance of adaptability. Life, with its unpredictability, can shake up even the most well-ordered habits. Whether it's a new job, a move to a different city, or a change in personal relationships, life events can disrupt your routines. Embracing flexibility isn't just about bouncing back from these disruptions; it's also about adapting your strategies to suit new circumstances. This might mean altering your morning routine or redefining what "success" looks like within your current context. Flexibility keeps your habits not only intact but relevant as you journey through different life stages.

Consider a support system as another backbone to sustaining habits over time. Just as plants may require a stake to grow straight and tall, habits often need the encouragement and accountability of others. Social interactions can bolster your efforts, providing perspective, motivation, and the occasional nudge when you're veering off track. Whether it's through online communities, friends, or family, surrounding yourself with a network that understands and supports your journey can enliven your commitment and make the process more rewarding.

It's also advantageous to periodically self-reflect, assessing how aligned your habits are with your evolving goals and values. As you grow, what you initially sought out of a habit might transform. Regular check-ins can guide whether to adjust, scale up, or perhaps even retire certain patterns. Reflective practices don't have to be elaborate. A simple weekly reflection journal, a meditative walk, or discussing your progress with a mentor can yield insights that foster deeper alignment between your actions and aspirations.

Now, let's talk about the influence of incremental rewards. Immediate gratifications often lure us into habits—think of the rush from a successful workout or completing a challenging project. But sustaining habits over the long haul benefits from small, consistent rewards. These can be as simple as acknowledging your progress or treating yourself to small pleasures after reaching milestone markers. Rewards can reinforce the behaviors you want to sustain, serving as constant reminders of why these habits matter in the fabric of your life.

One common challenge, though, is the monotony that sometimes creeps into our routines. Routine doesn't necessarily have to mean repetitive or boring. Introducing variation and novelty every so often can rejuvenate your commitment. This might mean taking a different path on your daily walks or experimenting with new productivity techniques. Refreshing your routine keeps your brain engaged and reminds you of the excitement and potential that new habits hold.

Visualizing the long-term impacts of your habits can also be a motivational tool for sustainability. Imagine the compounding benefits that come from consistently saving a small amount of money, reading just a few pages each day, or dedicating time regularly to learning a new skill. These cumulative effects can be profound. Keeping your eyes on the horizon helps maintain perspective on why you started these habits in the first place and where they might lead.

Equally important is understanding setbacks as an inherent component of any long-term journey. They're not signs of failure but rather opportunities for growth and learning. When habits falter, rather than succumbing to frustration, analyze what led to the disruption. Was it due to an external distraction, or did an emotional factor play a role? Gleaning insights from these situations can refine your strategies, making your habits resilient and your efforts more meaningful.

Ultimately, sustaining beneficial habits over time demands commitment, but also compassion towards oneself. Breaking free from the rigid expectations and allowing space for life's imperfections can humanize the process. It's about finding a balance, knowing when to push forward, and when to gently step back. Over the long haul, sustaining habits becomes less about achieving perfection every day and more about crafting a life steeped in growth, aligned with values, and full of meaningful progress.

This sustained effort requires a holistic approach, weaving together motivation, discipline, adaptability, support, reflection, rewards, and self-compassion. On this journey, you'll find that although habits start as small individual actions, over time, they become the very foundations upon which your personal and professional growth is built, nurturing you into an ever-evolving version of yourself.

Adapting to Life Changes

Life is a series of constant changes, and our ability to adapt determines our success and well-being. Long-term maintenance of beneficial habits requires flexibility and a willingness to adjust when faced with life's unpredictable challenges. Whether transitioning to a new job or adjusting to significant life events like becoming a parent, the key is learning how to tweak your habits without losing sight of your goals. Change might seem daunting at first, but it also provides opportunities for growth and resilience.

The first step in adapting is acknowledging that change is inevitable. Our routines and habits give structure to our lives, but they shouldn't be so rigid that they crumble under the slightest pressure. Flexibility allows habits to evolve alongside us. Imagine a sapling bending in the wind rather than a dry branch that snaps. This pliability is what keeps us from breaking when life's tempests arise.

Consider the scenario of relocating to a new city. Such a move can disrupt even the most ingrained habits, and the familiar routines we rely on for daily stability might dissolve overnight. Yet, this disruption can also be seen as an opportunity to reevaluate and reshape habits deliberately. We can create new routines that are more aligned with the current phase of our life. This transition might require an initial investment of time and energy, but the payoff in personal growth and renewed clarity can be substantial.

It's vital to maintain a mindset of curiosity and openness during such times. One effective strategy is to view change as a learning experience rather than an obstacle. Ask yourself questions like, "What can I learn from this change?" or "How can this new situation help me grow?" This approach shifts the narrative from being a victim of circumstance to becoming an active participant in your own story.

Adapting to life changes also involves understanding the need for temporary adjustments in your expectations. When a new parent returns home with their newborn, the old schedule might just not fit anymore. Trying to maintain a pre-baby lifestyle could lead to frustration and burnout. Instead, it's crucial to adapt the goals and expectations around the newborn's schedule and needs. It doesn't mean giving up on personal goals but adjusting the path and the timeframes to accommodate new realities.

Moreover, effective adaptation often requires us to reassess our priorities. During transitional periods, certain aspects of life might take precedence over others. When this happens, we need to be honest with ourselves about what's most important at the moment and focus on habits that support those priorities. This might mean letting go of certain routines that don't contribute to current goals, thus freeing up cognitive and emotional space for more relevant habits.

An adaptive mindset also includes leveraging support systems. No person is an island, and during times of change, the encouragement and feedback of friends, family, or mentors can be invaluable. Engaging with supportive communities or seeking advice from experienced individuals can offer new perspectives and help ease the transition. It's not just about asking for help; it's also about receiving insights that can help shape and improve our approach to habit change.

Another tool in adjusting habits is technology. In today's digital age, numerous apps and digital platforms can help us track changes, set reminders, or even connect us with communities for support. These tools can be particularly helpful for maintaining accountability and consistency when the usual cues for our habits might be absent due to changes in our environment or routine.

Let's not forget the role of self-compassion in adapting to life changes. During periods of significant transition, we tend to be our own harshest critics. It's easy to fall into a trap of self-rebuke if things don't go as planned. Instead, extend the same kindness to yourself that you would to a friend in a similar situation. Recognize that stumbling is part of the process, and patience with yourself fosters resilience and perseverance.

Finally, reflection and adjustment are key components of maintaining long-term habit changes amidst life's unpredictability. Regularly taking time to assess what is working and what needs modification keeps us aligned with our evolving goals and circumstances. This reflective practice helps prevent small problems from escalating into significant setbacks, allowing more fluid integration of new habits as needed.

In essence, the capacity to adapt is not simply about reacting to external changes but anticipating them and adjusting proactively. It's about seeing every roadblock as a detour rather than an end. By cultivating flexibility and a growth-oriented outlook, we empower ourselves to not just survive change, but to thrive in it. Embracing change may begin with uncertainty, but it can lead to profound personal growth when approached with the right mindset and tools. After all, change is a catalyst for transformation, guiding us towards becoming more resilient and fully realized versions of ourselves.

Chapter 15: Customizing Your Habit Strategy

You've embarked on a transformative journey, evolving your habits to cultivate personal growth and productivity. Now, the one-size-fits-all approach fades, as it's time to tailor strategies to your unique rhythm and life. Customizing your habit strategy means identifying what resonates with you and fine-tuning your approach for success. It's all about embracing that singular blend of what drives you and what brings you joy, then using feedback as a compass for continuous improvement. Harness your insights and adapt your strategies not just to overcome obstacles, but to propel yourself toward the future you envision. This intrinsic empowerment forms the cornerstone of lasting transformation, ensuring that the habits you build today are the stepping stones to the person you aspire to become tomorrow.

Personalizing Approaches for Success

Embarking on the journey of personalizing your habit strategy requires a keen understanding of who you are and what you truly need. It's not a one-size-fits-all approach; it's a unique path forged by your values, goals, and personal circumstances. Personalization isn't merely about tweaking habits here and there; it's about aligning your daily actions with your life's philosophy. Consider your priorities, the pace of your life, and the environment you thrive in. These factors serve as the compass guiding your habit strategy.

In the quest to create a customized habit strategy, it's essential to recognize the behavioral patterns that define you. Reflect on what has and hasn't worked in the past. What habits have you tried to implement, and what were the outcomes? When you take the time to dissect the history of your habits, you learn more about your triggers, your responses, and the rewards that drive you. This self-awareness is the cornerstone of personalization.

Next, think about the intricacies of your existing lifestyle—your work commitments, familial responsibilities, and leisure activities. Each aspect of your life interacts with your habits, either facilitating or hindering them. Habits that don't align with your lifestyle often lead to friction and frustration. Strike a balance by introducing new routines that enhance, rather than disrupt, the flow of your daily activities. Ask yourself: Does this habit fit into the rhythm of my life?

Setting realistic expectations is another crucial component. It's tempting to overhaul your life overnight, but sustainable change is gradual. Start small, focusing on one habit at a time. Break down your goals into manageable steps. As you experience success, you'll not only build confidence but also develop a system of reward and reinforcement that is personal to you. Celebrate small victories to fuel your momentum, acknowledging each step forward.

Now, think about your motivations. What drives you to want change? Intrinsic motivation, the kind that comes from within—such as personal growth or a deep desire for change— tends to be more sustainable than external rewards. Reflect on your intrinsic motivations and tie your new habits to these deeper values. Personalizing your habit strategy means crafting a life that resonates with your core identity.

Consider tailoring your environment to support your habits. We're deeply influenced by our surroundings, often more than we realize. Make deliberate choices about how you organize your space. Eliminate distractions, introduce cues that trigger the desired behavior, and create an atmosphere that reinforces your new habits. Personalization extends not only to the habits themselves but to the settings in which they occur.

Feedback is a valuable tool in this process. Regularly assess what's working and what isn't. Use feedback as a means to refine and adjust. Remember, personalization is a dynamic process involving continuous improvement. Habit trackers or journals can be an effective way to monitor progress and gather data about your patterns. They act as mirrors reflecting your journey, helping you decide which paths to pursue further and which to abandon.

Accountability is another element to incorporate into your strategy. While this might seem external, understanding your personal accountability style can enhance personalization. For some, simply knowing they have to report to someone (even if it's themselves) can be motivating. Others thrive on self-driven efforts. Select an accountability method that fits your personality, whether it's sharing your goals with a friend, using a habit-tracking app, or keeping a daily log.

Also, openness to experimentation can not be understated. Try different approaches, and don't be afraid to adjust as you uncover methods that don't suit your nature. You may find that a morning routine is more effective than an evening one, or that visual cues work better than reminders on your phone. Each failure or success adds another piece to the puzzle of your ideal strategy.

Lastly, nurture self-compassion throughout this process. Personalizing your habit strategy involves vulnerability and courage, but it also requires patience and kindness toward yourself. There will be setbacks. It's important to treat each misstep as a learning experience rather than a failure. This forgiving mindset encourages resilience, making you more likely to succeed in the long run.

In summary, personalizing approaches for success is about crafting a lifestyle that is uniquely suited to you—a seamless blend of your ideals, your daily actions, and your overarching goals. It's about becoming the architect of your habitual journey, ensuring that every structure you build is sturdy and aligned with the essence of who you are. Through reflection, adjustment, and compassion, you can create a habit strategy that leads to profound growth and enduring success.

Utilizing Feedback for Continuous Improvement

Creating an effective habit strategy tailored to your unique needs is a journey, not a one-off task. Personal growth and productivity improvements stem from the continual refinement of this strategy. At the heart of this process is feedback—a powerful tool that can illuminate the path forward. When used wisely, feedback provides clarity, drives motivation, and highlights both strengths and areas needing development. It's essential in crafting a habit strategy that isn't just customized at the outset but is fine-tuned over time.

Feedback, in this context, doesn't strictly refer to comments or evaluations from others but encompasses self-reflection and assessment of your own progress. This internal feedback can be as simple as noting your feelings or energy levels after engaging in a particular routine. Are you invigorated or drained? Does the habit align with your long-term goals, or is it veering you off course? By regularly tuning in to these personal cues, you create a loop of continuous improvement—a cycle where you act, reflect, adjust, and improve.

Moreover, feedback involves recognizing and celebrating successes, no matter how small. Each small victory on your habit formation journey is a testament to your commitment and determination. Acknowledging these wins not only boosts confidence but also fortifies your motivation to continue. Positive reinforcement is a strong ally in creating habit changes that stick. And as your self-awareness grows, so does your ability to modify your habits for the better.

On the other hand, identifying setbacks or discrepancies in your habit strategy is equally crucial. It is in these moments of reflection that true growth often occurs. Ask yourself: What triggered a lapse or deviation from your routine? Was it a lack of resources, time, or perhaps unrealistic expectations? Digging deep to understand these triggers provides actionable insights that can transform stumbling blocks into stepping stones.

One effective method to harness feedback is through journaling. By documenting your experiences, challenges, and triumphs, you create a tangible record of your journey. This practice allows for regular review and deeper understanding. Over time, patterns emerge—both positive and negative—and equip you with the knowledge necessary to fine-tune your habits for desired outcomes. Importantly, journaling can serve as a reflective mirror, offering perspectives you might miss during the hustle of everyday life.

External feedback, coming from friends, family, mentors, or coaches, can also be invaluable. These perspectives can offer a fresh angle, sometimes uncovering blind spots you may not see. However, it's essential to approach this type of feedback constructively. Recognize that while others can offer insights, the ultimate decision about which adjustments to make lies with you. You hold the reins on your habit transformation journey, and any feedback should align with your personal goals and values.

It's crucial to maintain a mindset of openness and curiosity when receiving feedback. Defensive reactions can stifle growth, while openness fosters learning and adaptation. Consider each piece of feedback as a puzzle piece, potentially fitting into the larger picture of your habit strategy. It might be challenging to hear that a particular routine isn't yielding the anticipated results, but such revelations are opportunities to innovate and pivot.

Equally important is filtering the feedback you receive. Not every piece of advice or critique will be relevant or beneficial. Staying grounded in your goals and recognizing the distinction between constructive input and unnecessary noise can save time and energy. This discernment ensures that the feedback you integrate into your strategy is beneficial and aligns with your values and aspirations.

Incorporating feedback isn't a passive act; it's an active, dynamic process. It involves setting aside time for reflection, asking critical questions, and being willing to experiment and tweak your approach. In this way, feedback becomes a catalyst for creativity and innovation in your habit strategy. The adaptability you cultivate through this process is an invaluable skill, fostering resilience and readiness in the face of inevitable changes that life may present.

To truly harness feedback for continuous improvement, it's essential to foster a culture of experimentation. Try viewing your habit-building efforts as a series of experiments. Not every attempt will thrive, and that's perfectly okay. What matters is the willingness to tweak and try again the moment something doesn't work as expected. This spirit of experimentation keeps the process fresh and engaging, preventing stagnation and maintaining momentum toward your goals.

Additionally, consider setting regular intervals for formal feedback review—be it weekly, monthly, or quarterly. During these reviews, compare your actual progress with the milestones you've set. Evaluate which strategies are working, which aren't, and why. This structured approach ensures you don't become complacent and that your habits are continuously aligned with your evolving objectives.

Ultimately, utilizing feedback for continuous improvement requires commitment and patience. It's a lifelong journey where self-awareness and external input blend to sculpt your habits into powerful tools for personal development. Every piece of feedback, whether it reassures or challenges you, contributes to a deeper understanding of yourself and your goals. As you grow more adept at incorporating this feedback, you learn not just how to change your habits, but how to transform your life with intention and foresight.

Conclusion

As we journey through life, the quest for personal growth and improved productivity remains a constant endeavor. Habits are an integral part of this journey, serving as both foundations and bridges as we move from one stage of personal development to the next. Mastering these habits equips us with the tools we need to write our story and live it authentically.

In our exploration, we've dissected the psychology behind why habits form, examined the science of change, and delved into practical strategies for overcoming resistance. We've seen how habits can be leveraged for productivity and aligned with personal goals to support a growth mindset. Through understanding and harnessing the power of habits, we recognize they're not just routines to be mindlessly followed; they're deliberate actions that can transform our lives in profound ways.

Picture your future self, intentionally crafting a life that reflects your deepest values and aspirations. The path to becoming this version of yourself is rooted in the habits you cultivate today. Every small step counts, from setting beneficial routines to tackling internal obstacles and managing the inevitable setbacks along the way. In a world that often glorifies instant results, remember that meaningful change unfolds over time, woven into the fabric of our daily actions.

Environmental factors and social influences play pivotal roles in shaping our habits, reminding us of the importance of creating spaces and communities that support our journeys. By minimizing distractions, leveraging peer support, and navigating negative influences, we cultivate an environment ripe for transformation. The insights gained from these experiences underscore a central truth: change doesn't happen in isolation. It is a collective, dynamic process influenced by the company we keep and the environment we shape.

Throughout this book, real-life stories of habit transformation have illustrated the power of persistence, adaptability, and resilience. These narratives reveal that success isn't linear— it's a mosaic of attempts, failures, adjustments, and triumphs. They inspire us to see our setbacks not as dead-ends but as opportunities for learning and growth.

Tracking progress and making adjustments are vital components of this journey. With the right tools, we can monitor habits objectively and make informed changes to enhance our quality of life. Adaptability becomes a key strength, allowing us to sustain beneficial habits even as life's circumstances evolve. This adaptability underscores the importance of customizing our strategies for personal success. By utilizing feedback effectively, continuous improvement becomes not just possible, but inevitable.

Finally, as our exploration of habit mastery culminates, we embrace the truth that personal development is a lifelong venture. Each chapter of your life calls for a reevaluation of habits, a reimagining of possibilities, and a renewed commitment to growth. This ongoing process requires patience, self-compassion, and a willingness to recalibrate when necessary. Imagine a future where your habits align seamlessly with who you are and where you wish to be. This vision isn't just attainable; it is within your grasp as you apply the principles and insights shared throughout this book.

In conclusion, remember that the power to transform your habits lies within you. Armed with knowledge, strategies, and inspiration, you stand ready to craft the life you've envisioned—one thoughtful habit at a time. So go forth with confidence, knowing that each choice you make contributes to the tapestry of your extraordinary life.

Appendix A: Appendix

The journey we've embarked on through the art of habits uncovers the profound interconnectedness between our daily actions and long-term ambitions. As you've explored each chapter, identifying patterns and implementing changes, this appendix serves as a map to review key insights, strategies, and principles that have been woven throughout the book.

The effectiveness of mastering habits lies not just in understanding theory but in practical application. By now, you may have realized that change starts with small, intentional steps. These aren't meant to overhaul your world overnight but to create a ripple effect, gradually transforming your habits from weak foundations to pillars of personal strength and growth.

Remember, it's the consistent actions, even those seemingly insignificant, that compound over time, ultimately leading to significant improvement in your personal and professional life. Empowering yourself with this knowledge gives you the courage to tackle any habits that no longer serve you.

Navigating the complexities of habit change requires mindfulness and a genuine understanding of the psychology behind why we do what we do. Through distinctive behavior patterns, our environment, and the influences of those around us, these elements play vital roles in either propelling you forward or holding you back. It's up to you to harness their power wisely.

The stories shared throughout this book aim to inspire and show you that you're not alone in this pursuit of self-betterment. Each narrative illustrates the diversity of experiences and the common thread of perseverance through setbacks and triumphs alike. Take these stories as reminders that every journey is unique, and personal growth knows no universal trajectory.

In conclusion, as you continue to craft your narrative, realize that the canvas of your life is ever-evolving. With the right tools, a resilient mindset, and an unwavering commitment to betterment, you hold the brush that paints your future, stroke by meticulous stroke. With each habit you refine and each goal you approach with clarity, you're not just changing habits; you're transforming your life in ways that resonate well beyond the mundane.

As you revisit these reflections, let them be both a comforting guide and a call to action. Embrace the process of continuous evaluation and adaptation. With the strategies and insights gathered within these pages, you're equipped to not only achieve success but also to sustain and grow it throughout the journey of life.